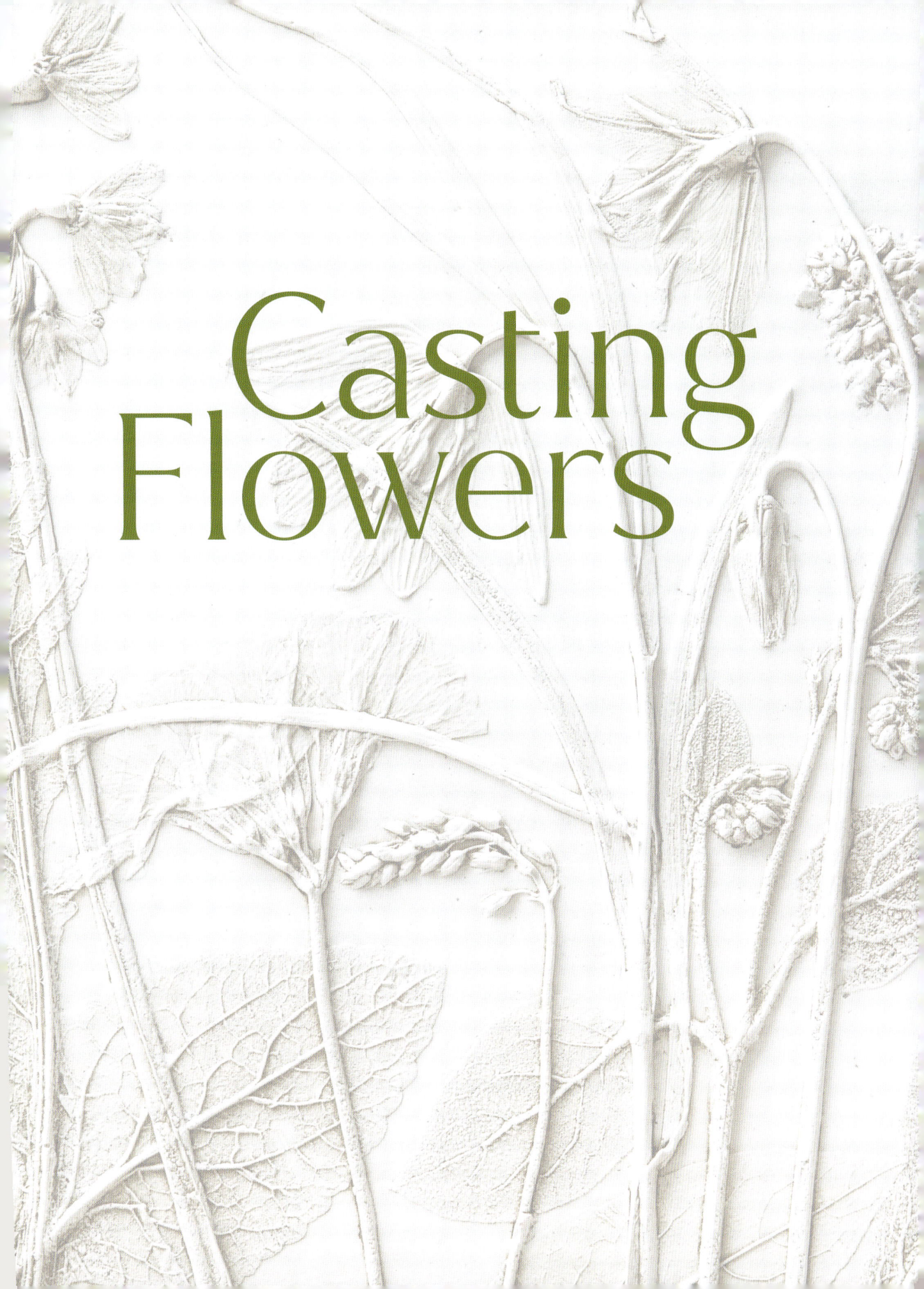

Casting Flowers

Casting Flowers

A Step-by-Step Guide to Creating Beautiful Botanical Art

Rachel Dein
with Juliet Roberts

Photography by Éva Németh

Timber Press
Portland, OR

Timber Press
Workman Publishing
Hachette Book Group, Inc.
1290 Avenue of the Americas
New York, New York 10104
timberpress.com

Timber Press is an imprint of Workman Publishing, a division of Hachette Book Group,
Inc. The Timber Press name and logo are registered trademarks of Hachette Book
Group, Inc.

Printed in China on responsibly sourced paper
Text and cover design by Leigh Thomas
Page 14: Folio 197 verso, Ambrosiana Library Milan (ambrosiana.it/en)
Page 15: Linnean Society Library, London (linnean.org)

The publisher is not responsible for websites (or their content) that are not owned
by the publisher.

The Hachette Speakers Bureau provides a wide range of authors for speaking
events. To find out more, go to hachettespeakersbureau.com or email
hachettespeakers@hbgusa.com.

ISBN 978-1-64326-346-5

A catalog record for this book is available from the Library of Congress.

Contents

A Word from the Artist

—

Plants have always been very important to me, and I love gathering them from my garden in London.

> "Snatching the eternal out of the desperately fleeting is the great magic trick of human existence."
>
> —Tennessee Williams

I am an artist who loves casting, and I also love the natural world of plants and flowers. There's a long history of people making impressions from nature; however, after having done some quite extensive research, I believe that the techniques I have developed for casting impressions of plants and flowers are unique. My work—which I call botanical bas-relief—is the culmination of my life as an artist and a prop maker over the past thirty years.

In 1989, aged twenty, I began working toward a degree in fine art at Middlesex Polytechnic in North London, where we were mainly left to our own devices. For the first few months, without any structure and not much to say as an artist, I pretty much floundered. The things that I'd always enjoyed about art, including drawing and sculpting from life, were frowned upon by those around me, so I ended up joining everyone else in being a bit more conceptual and experimental. I focused on playing around with plants and photography, which were always interests of mine.

I liked the work of British sculptor, photographer, and environmentalist Andy Goldsworthy, who produces site-specific sculpture situated in natural and urban settings. Photography plays a crucial role in his art due to the often ephemeral and transient state of his pieces. According to Goldsworthy, "Each work grows, stays, decays—integral parts of a cycle which the photograph shows at its height, marking the moment when the work is most alive."

I began casting in plaster as an art student in North London and have never ceased to enjoy this wonderful process.

At the end of my first year, disaster struck when I was told that someone very close to me was seriously ill and was going to die. Yet, somehow, after a miserable time contemplating mortality and loss, I finally found my voice as an artist. I drew on a childhood memory of throwing a handful of melon seeds down the bathroom sink, only to discover, some weeks later, plants growing up and out of the overflow. It seemed to encapsulate everything I wanted to express. It showed me how tough and tenacious nature is, which I found profoundly comforting.

At the time, I was reading the novel *One Hundred Years of Solitude* by Gabriel García Márquez. The author included many descriptions of ruins overrun with plants, which also reinforced this message. I started to grow plants in unusual places, such as amongst the bristles of a toothbrush and through the upholstery of furniture. From here, I started to carve furniture out of vegetables. For me, the furniture represented people, and I filmed the process of decay using stop motion. As the vegetables dried up and changed shape, the camera caught them "coming alive".

Then came my discovery of casting in plaster. I'd signed up for a short class in glass blowing, where we were taught to press shapes into wet sand and then pour molten glass into the hollow spaces—a basic but effective way of casting in glass. I went back to my studio and started experimenting with pressing objects into clay and casting them by pouring plaster into the resulting voids. I was amazed and fascinated by the detail achieved.

After leaving college, I briefly took on a studio, which appropriately was a disused fruit and veg shop in Spitalfields Market, London. This, however, didn't last long, as I needed to earn money. I was fortunate to get an apprenticeship as a prop maker at the English National Opera, and this was the start of my prop-making career, which I loved, as I was being paid to paint and sculpt! I worked freelance for fifteen years for different theatres and museums, including Madame Tussauds, the Royal Opera House, Shakespeare's Globe, and various West End theatres.

After five years working as a freelance prop maker, I was given the opportunity to have a studio space for six months. I continued with the materials and subject matter that had interested me before. I was drawn to the stories of Frankenstein and the golem—of man attempting to create "life". I began carving human features into potatoes—mouths, brows of faces, and hands. Again, I filmed them using time-lapse/stop motion, as I was interested in what they might "say" as they moved. Following on from hands, I used chicken feet, which I manipulated into different human gestures—begging, praying, and swearing. I then cast them into plaster. Using 102 chicken feet manipulated into different positions of British Sign Language, I spelt out "In the beginning was the Word, and the Word was with God, and the Word was God." I was trying to show what

we are other than just flesh, and what animal matter is compared to vegetable matter, and then what human is compared to animal. Looking back now, I can see how these two interests of using natural materials and casting, as well as my continuing interest in capturing the ephemeral, have fed into my current work.

In 2001, I became a mother and continued to work part-time; however, my life as a prop maker ended when my third child came along. When my youngest started school in 2010, I started making again in a studio space I'd created in the loft of my home.

I first created castings under the name Tactile Studio. I used this name for a few years but eventually decided to use my own name. A local church invited creative people in the area to show their work, and it was here that someone from a gallery saw my tiles and invited me to exhibit. My first commission soon followed. A lady who'd bought one of my small tiles asked me to make a family portrait comprising favourite things belonging to her, her husband, and their children.

This commission made me realise that I'd always wanted to preserve my wedding bouquet, and though the original flowers were long gone, I could try and replicate it. In 2011, a lovely florist's shop opened at the end of my road. I went in to buy spring flowers similar to those I'd used in my wedding bouquet eight years earlier. The manager of the flower shop was curious to know what I was

When I started making casts of various bits and bobs such as toys, doll's dresses, pine cones, and shells, my aim was to make little gifts that I could sell at local markets.

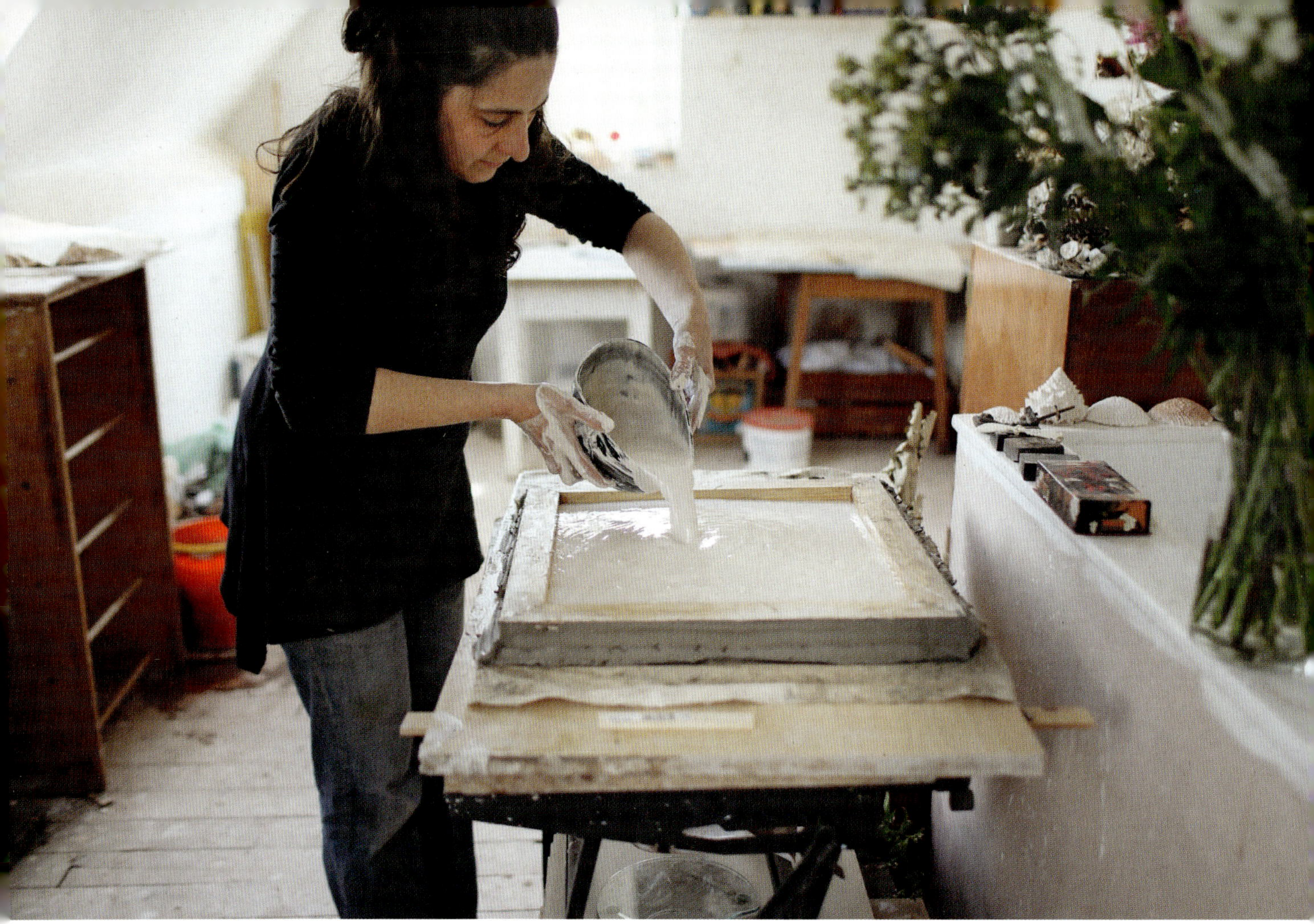

The *Gardenista* design blog featured my work in 2012—the first of numerous other editorial features.

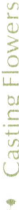

doing, so I showed her some images of my work, and she kindly began giving me flowers for free that she couldn't sell. I was pleased with the results of my bouquet castings, and not long afterwards, I began to sell my work. Unwittingly, this was the catalyst for the botanical work I still love making today.

In 2013, I was invited by a friend to attend the Royal Horticultural Society Chelsea Flower Show. While we were there, I realised this could be the perfect place to show my work, so I applied for a trade stand. This was a very large gamble–the cost was equivalent to a fancy family holiday, as well as a lot of childcare favours–but it paid off. I've had a stand at Chelsea for the past ten years.

In the summer of 2016, the BBC television programme *Countryfile* invited me to make casts out and about in the countryside. This prompted the Chelsea Physic Garden in London to suggest that I make bas-relief castings of the medicinal plants in their collection. Shortly afterwards, I was contacted by the events team of Raymond Blanc's pop-up restaurant, Jardin Blanc. They asked me to create pieces for them to display at the 2017 RHS Chelsea Flower Show. As a teenager, I'd been hugely impressed by a special family outing to Le Manoir aux Quat'Saisons, Blanc's famous restaurant in Oxfordshire, and I still have a photo of me taken in the garden there. I suggested that I cast the edible plants and flowers grown in the kitchen garden, and they agreed, kindly giving me access to whatever I wanted to use there, and this is how my *Le Manoir* collection came about.

I have also been commissioned to create work for some large-scale projects, including the flagship London store of luxury brand Huishan Zhang in Mount Street, Mayfair; HIDE, a restaurant in Piccadilly; twenty-six panels for a hallway in Montana; a ceiling for a house in Wisconsin; and a year-long series for the iconic garden Hidcote in Gloucestershire, which culminated in an exhibition in 2019. More recently, I have created a series of large panels for the dining area of the MS *Iona*, a cruise ship in the P&O Cruises fleet.

As well as various exhibitions, some exciting spin-offs have resulted. In 2018, Area Environments, a wall-covering company in Minnesota, added some of my pieces to their portfolio of artists whose work they scale up and then print onto wallpaper. I made a piece for the Bryant Family Vineyard in California, which was copied and embossed into the paper that lines the gift box for a very special vintage. The Wellbeing Garden at RHS Wisley asked me to make concrete pieces that were designed to be touched, for visually impaired visitors. Dutch garden designer Carien van Boxtel commissioned some bas-relief bricks that were incorporated into the path of her cut-flower garden at the RHS Hampton Court Palace Garden Festival. In 2022–23, I collaborated with the head gardener at the National Trust's Nunnington Hall in Yorkshire, casting the plants throughout the year for an exhibition at the sixteenth-century manor house.

My process is deceptively simple. I arrange and press flowers and foliage into clay. Once the plants are removed from the clay, I place a wooden frame on the clay and pour in the plaster, which is allowed to set. I then peel away the clay and push the plaster cast out of its frame. Then I wash off most of the surface clay, leaving traces to enhance the details.

It is my hope that this book provides you with the tools you need to implement botanical bas-reliefs on your own. I love the process deeply, and it is a pleasure to share it with you in the form of this book.

Botanical Bas-Relief and the Origins of Nature Printing

1

The director of the Horta Museum in Brussels bought some of my pieces in 2014. She told me that she had a collection of nineteenth-century plaster casts of plants that were similar to my work. However, when she sent me some photos, it was clear that these were sculpted plants and fruits, not casts from actual plants. This correspondence, along with an invitation to speak at Gardens Illustrated Festival 2015 in southern England, ignited my curiosity to explore precedents for my botanical bas-reliefs. After extensive research, I could find no prior examples of impressions of plants being cast in plaster or concrete. The only thing that came anywhere close was nature printing, a technique in which prints are made directly from the natural object itself.

Casting in plaster to make replicas is thought to date back to the Roman Empire and even ancient Egypt. However, the process I use for making casts of plants is new. My botanical bas-reliefs are based on the sculpture technique in which the details of figures and/or other design elements are just barely more prominent than the background.

Making prints from nature is a far older practice. The earliest examples are the human handprints found in cave dwellings, with the oldest instances believed to be red ochre hand stencils in the Cave of Maltravieso, in Cáceres, Spain. Made by Neanderthals, the seventy-one hand stencils have been dated to the prehistoric era more than 64,000 years ago (predating the arrival of our modern human ancestors, *Homo sapiens*, in Europe by some 20,000 years).

Leonardo da Vinci described
the process of nature printing
and featured a single sage leaf
by way of illustration in *Codex
Atlanticus*.

The earliest known botanical print is of two leaves, believed to be made in the year 1228 AD by Bihnam the Christian, in a copy of a manuscript written by Greek physician, pharmacologist, and botanist Pedanius Dioscorides (circa 40–90 AD). Almost 300 years after this first nature print was made, Leonardo da Vinci (1452–1519) described the process of taking an impression from nature in his *Codex Atlanticus* (*Codice Atlantico*), a twelve-volume set of drawings and writings published in the sixteenth century. The work contains a botanical print of a single sage leaf, which I particularly like because it's timeless, simple, and indistinguishable from the sage-leaf casts that I make now.

The interest in both medicinal and useful plants continued to grow during the following centuries, and the ability to identify particular specimens scientifically became increasingly important, in particular for professional groups such as apothecaries, botanists, plant hunters, and perfumiers. In the early 1800s, further technical progress was made with printing presses, and paper production was mechanized, making it cheaper to produce. This helped pave the way for the large-scale production of nature prints.

With the advent of photography and increasingly sophisticated methods of printing, nature printing fell into decline. Today, taking direct impressions from the natural world is more likely to be employed by artists, and this simple technique has indeed been combined with numerous other printing techniques to create a huge variety of beautiful images.

I like to think of botanical bas-relief as a contemporary form of creating fossils: it captures moments in time in plaster or concrete rather than rock. Like those ancient relics, these new images have a poetry all their own. For me, they

Examples of nature printing have been found in the correspondence sent by Swedish scientist Olaf Celsius (1670–1756) to his friend and mentee, Swedish botanist Carl Linnaeus (1707–1778).

fulfil a deep desire to capture the ephemeral in the natural world and celebrate the beauty and fleeting quality of life itself.

It can be hugely pleasurable to look at plants in detail, and though I'm not an artist who makes work about environmental issues, I'm keen to see more people connect with nature. My feeling is that if you love something, there's a better chance that you will care about it. It is my hope that more people will enjoy making botanical bas-reliefs. Whether their creations are for themselves, for gifts, or for sale, I hope that they get as much pleasure out of both the process and the end results as I do.

How to Use
This Book

have developed a remarkably straightforward, accessible, rewarding—even magical—technique for making botanical bas-relief casts, and I'm intrigued to see how different people around the world respond to and develop it. In particular, I wonder how it will speak to sculptors, ceramic artists, and others who use clay. As well as being beautiful art forms for their own sake, botanical bas-reliefs hold endless possibilities for more practical uses. What might traditional plasterers and interior designers create for their various projects? Children often have boundless creativity, and I'm extremely interested in what new things they may come up with.

This book contains all the information you need to make a botanical bas-relief. Following are a list of questions that I've been asked over the years, which I hope will resolve any queries readers may have.

Who can do this technique?

Botanical bas-relief is a simple process, and pretty much anyone from around five years upwards (albeit with some assistance) can have a go at it. It's relatively inexpensive, too, so you don't need tons of money to do it. Also, horticultural therapists have told me that it's a wonderful activity for their patients with physical disabilities or mental health issues.

What should I know before starting?

This technique is fun, rewarding, and remarkably straightforward. This book will give you all the necessary information and advice you need to get started. Begin with small, easy projects, such as a sage-leaf casting, and gain confidence before attempting bigger, more complex castings. As with many things, practise makes perfect, so don't think that your first work will necessarily be your best. Remember to keep notes and learn from your mistakes, but most of all, just keep practising!

Do I need to have a garden?

You don't need to have your own garden. In my experience, it's fairly easy to find interesting plants wherever you live; it's just a matter of focusing on plants that will give good results, so take a good look around you. I've found interesting specimens on verges and hedges in the city and on country hikes. I've also been given flowers from friends and neighbours. If all else fails, you can buy flowers and stems from florists or even supermarkets.

What if I'm not very artistic?

There is no need to be able to draw, and you can get lovely results whatever your capabilities. Plants are invariably so beautiful that it's almost impossible to go wrong. Anyone who can follow a simple recipe can make a botanical bas-relief.

Is it expensive to buy the materials and equipment?

The outlay for equipment and materials is relatively modest, and if your budget is tight, you can improvise in many ways. For example, I found a long, cylindrical piece of wood in a dumpster, and I use that as my largest rolling pin. It's always worth asking a local wood supplier for any offcuts that you could use for a rolling pin, as a board to work on, or to make a frame. Ask friends and family if they have any wood scraps to give you. If you don't have a piece of wood to use as a board, you can use a plastic chopping board from the kitchen. If you can't find a flexible steel scraper, you could improvise with a metal ruler.

Can I use clay from the garden?

Yes, you can, though clay from the garden may be grittier and less smooth compared to shop-bought clay. Garden clay won't take in the plants' fine detail quite so well, but there is no reason you shouldn't have a go and see what results you get.

How much work surface do I need?

You don't need much space—just the size of a small table. In essence, you need enough room for the size of your work board and an area around it for your tools, and ideally enough space to pre-arrange your flowers. If you don't have a table or if space is tight, you could use a kitchen work surface or a sideboard. Again, think creatively and be flexible in your approach. If you're concerned about getting the surface wet or damaged, you can use thick plastic sheeting to protect it. It helps if your work surface is sturdy and relatively level, because it's important that the plaster sets to an equal depth in the frame so the piece doesn't end up lopsided.

What sort of work space do I need?

Ideally, your space will have good natural light, although you can work under artificial lighting. It helps if you can clearly see what you're doing! You don't need a faucet and sink where you are working, but they are helpful when you clean the piece. That said, you can always improvise with a bucket or bowl of water or an outside faucet.

Can I do the process standing up or do I need to sit down?

You can sit down to do much of the process, but I invariably stand because it's easier to push the rolling pin when flattening the clay and I get a better overview when laying out the plants. Obviously, if you are creating a small botanical bas-relief, sitting down to work is fine, but you may need to stand to work on bigger pieces.

Is it a messy process? Should I wear protective clothing?

You can wear perfectly nice clothes and an apron. If you get any marks from the clay on your clothes, you can simply wash them off. That said, red (terracotta) clay is a bit more difficult to remove than grey clay. Dried plaster is fairly easy to pick off fabric. It may be worthwhile to remove any rings, bracelets, and, in particular, watches, because they can get in your way. In theory, making a silicone mould shouldn't be messy, but silicone doesn't come off fabric, so I recommend wearing an apron or work clothes when working with silicone. Better to be safe than sorry!

My studio space is situated in my attic, which offers good light and enough space to keep my tools, equipment, and materials as well as silicone moulds I've made over the years.

How long does it take to create a bas-relief from start to finish?

It's tricky to say, as much depends on the size of the casting, how many plants you are using, where you are gathering them from, and how decisive you are when arranging. After you have everything in place, including tools, materials, and plants, it could take approximately two hours, including time for the plaster to dry.

Can I do this with my kids?

Yes; though the ideal age would be around ten years old, even a child as young as five can create a bas-relief with some assistance. Much depends on the child's temperament and ability. I often made plaster casts with my children when they were young, and they really enjoyed it. The process is rewarding when you're working alone but great fun when working with friends and family.

Is there anything dangerous or toxic in the process?

The process isn't dangerous. However, I recommend using a protective dust mask and goggles when mixing the plaster. Some plants can be toxic, so either avoid using them or wear suitable protection.

Getting Started:
How to Cast a
Botanical Bas-Relief

3

Making a botanical bas-relief is a magical process. Because I'm a keen gardener and really enjoy working with plants, I think of it as casting the garden itself. All of my work is part of an ongoing experiment, and, even now, I accept the fact that some pieces will be successful and some won't. If I'm not a fan of a cast I've made, I put it to one side. When I come back to it, I often discover new qualities in the work. Imperfection is part of the beauty of nature, and it is integral to my artistic process.

Once the plants are removed from the clay, the impressions left behind may seem messy or unclear; my advice is to see the process through. I find that, despite my worries, the cast usually becomes a pretty accurate replica. There's a sort of diaphanous transparency to the end result, almost as if you can see the three-dimensionality of the plants in X-ray form, and it can be difficult to imagine this when you place the plants on the clay.

I'm a sort of court painter or portrait photographer. I can go to a garden and capture a specific moment in time, or I can cast the flowers to commemorate a special event such as a wedding, birthday, funeral, or anniversary. It feels important to create a record of significant and meaningful moments, whether that involves flowers or personal objects. All moments are ephemeral, and objects can get lost in time. Someone recently said to me that they found my work very calming, and in many ways, I think I'm creating it as a form of self-soothing. The process of collecting plants and flowers, composing them, and casting helps keep me centered and gives me a feeling of balance and calm.

I love working with plants and enjoy having their beautiful forms and often lovely scents around the studio.

Over the years, I've refined my techniques, and I sometimes miss the rawness of my earlier pieces. Compared to when I first started, I am far more thorough at taking out every tiny bit of plant remaining in the clay, and I spend more time sanding the plaster. I don't always have time to play around with various compositions, but there can be something very liberating about just getting on with it. If one's expectations are too high, it can be a bit stifling. I always try to do my best, but the unexpected results often can be the most beautiful and rewarding. No one has the Midas touch. I encourage everyone simply to enjoy the process of creating and have fun playing with the flowers.

Set up your workspace

You don't need a lot of space—just enough room for a wooden board and an area around it for laying out your tools and setting out plants. It's important to have a clean workspace that is clear of clutter to allow for a calming and creative environment.

How to build a frame

Before you can cast, you need to create a frame that is deep enough to hold the plaster required for whatever size casting you're working on. The frames I use have mitred corners, but the frame you make using the method described here is easier to build. The finished frame measures 12 cm (4¾ in.) square. This frame is just one of several sizes that I like working with. Frame size and shape are very much a personal choice, so feel free to cut the wood accordingly.

It's important that you get the corners of the frame as square as possible. (My frames aren't perfectly square, but I embrace that asymmetry and enjoy them for being all the more idiosyncratic.) You could potentially use an old picture frame as long as it's deep enough to hold the plaster. It's always worth experimenting.

I have made a range of different sized square frames; you can make a frame in whatever size and shape you prefer.

Tools and materials for building a frame

- 4 pieces of wood: 2 measuring 21 cm × 4.5 cm (8 ¼ in. × 1¾ in.) and 2 measuring 12 cm × 4.5 cm (4¾ in. × 1¾ in.)

- ruler

- pencil

- handsaw

- tape

- right-angle tool (90-degree ruler, square ruler)

- drill and drill bits

- screwdriver/screwdriver attachment for drill

- 4 wood screws, 5 cm (2 in.) long

- wood glue (optional, because this frame is relatively small. For a bigger frame, using glue will help make the frame sturdier. If you don't use wood glue, you can release the cast by unscrewing the frame.)

To make a frame, you'll need a handsaw, wood, wood screws, and a screwdriver, among other items.

Instructions

1. Measure and cut your wood to size, making sure that the ends are square. I use 2.5 cm × 5 cm (1 in. × 2 in.) lumber, which is quite sturdy.

2. Position the two longest pieces opposite each other, and then put the two smaller sides in place to create the frame. If using wood glue, smear some on either ends of the two shorter pieces of wood.

3. Butt the ends of the wood pieces firmly together. Use tape to hold everything in place, if needed.

4. Pre-drill the holes for the screws, all the way through the top piece of wood and slightly into the piece to be attached. You need to be able to ease in the screw without splitting the wood.

5. Use a screwdriver or a power drill with a screwdriver attachment to sink one screw into each corner.

The edge of the frame, showing the screws in place

Casting in plaster

After you've assembled your tools, equipment, and materials, created a frame, and gathered your plants, you're ready to make a bas-relief.

Materials, tools, and equipment

If you're hoping to buy materials and tools locally, look for fine art and craft supply shops that stock clay, plaster, and silicone moulding kits. You may also find sculptor supply shops a good source for materials, including flexible steel scrapers. Builders' merchants will also stock plaster, wood, spirit (bubble) levels, and dust masks. You can find rolling pins and scissors at cookery supply shops and snips and secateurs (pruners) at gardening stores. It's also worth searching for your specific needs online.

Top left: Clockwise from upper left: dust mask, steel scrapers, signature stamp, hammer, wooden rolling pin, level, petroleum jelly, lint-free cloth, scissors, utility knife, scalpel blades

Top middle: From left: sandpaper roll, sponge, wood block, paintbrushes

Top right: Clockwise from upper left: plaster, jug of water, flexible rubber bowl

Bottom: Clockwise from top: wooden frame, hammer, wooden rolling pin, steel scraper, utility knife and scalpel blades, flat board with plastic and clay

Tools and materials for casting in plaster

- strong, flat work board wider than your chosen frame (wood or plastic; or use an old chopping board)
- sheet of thick plastic (to stop clay sticking to the board)
- grey clay
- wooden frame (see "How to build a frame" on page 25)
- wooden rolling pin (ideally as wide as the frame)
- 2 super-thin, flexible steel scrapers, about 5 cm × 23 cm (2 in. × 9 in.) and 0.38 mm thick
- scalpel blade
- hammer
- secateurs/scissors (for cutting stems)
- lint-free cloth

- tweezers (optional)
- petroleum jelly (to prepare frame)
- dust mask
- plaster of Paris
- flexible mixing bowl
- jug (for water)
- spirit (bubble) level
- small bits of wood (to use as chocks, if needed)
- thick towel
- kitchen sponge and brushes in various sizes (for cleanup)
- sandpaper of various grits: 80, 120, 180, 320
- sanding block

Instructions

1. Cover the work board with thick plastic and place it on a flat, level table or work surface.

2. Place a lump of clay in the centre of the board. (See "Measuring the clay" (page 46) for information about how much clay to use.) Using the rolling pin, smash the clay to flatten it.

3a. Roll the clay into a slab approximately 20–40 mm (¾–1½ in.) wider than your frame.

3b. The thickness of the clay depends on the thickness of the plants you intend to use. I suggest a minimum clay depth of about 5 mm (¼ in.). Try to roll the clay as flat and as evenly as possible.

4a. Smooth the surface of the clay with the flexible steel scraper.

4b. Keep the scraper clean by using a second scraper to remove any clay.

5. If you spot air bubbles on the surface of the clay, use the point of the scalpel blade to pierce them and roll the clay smooth afterwards. If you leave air bubbles

in the clay, they will leave marks in the casting, so it is better to remove them at this stage.

6. Position the frame centred on the clay. Using a hammer, gently tap the frame down to make a faint impression on the clay's surface (a maximum of 1 mm is fine). This provides the outline in which you'll arrange the plants.

7. Lift off the frame and place it to the side.

8. Choose and arrange your plants, making sure that the composition works well within the outline of the frame. Use secateurs to cut stems to size. Depending on the size and varieties of plants you're using, you can either arrange them lightly on the clay or compose the arrangement to the side and then move it into the final position. I find it helpful to replace the frame every now and again to check that the arrangement sits nicely within it. Generally, I make sure that the ends of the stems extend over the bottom edge of the frame. This makes the composition appear more natural and makes it easier to lift plants out.

9. Once you are happy with the arrangement and it's sitting lightly on the clay, use your fingers to press the flowers, leaves, and stems gently into position in the clay. This helps minimise the possibility of plants moving around when you use the rolling pin to flatten them into the clay.

10a. Starting from the middle of the composition, pass the rolling pin over the plants to flatten and embed them into the clay. Press down relatively firmly on the rolling pin. First roll upwards, then downwards, and then side to side. If you start rolling from the very bottom or top of the composition, there's a chance the plants will shift out of position.

10b. As you work, be mindful to keep the rolling pin as clean as possible, checking it each time before you pass it over the clay. The rolling pin will get covered with sticky clay, so you'll need to scrape off excess clay regularly with a metal scraper.

10c. Bits of plant debris can also stick to the rolling pin, and you don't want to roll these bits back into the clay. Use a lint-free cloth to wipe down the rolling pin and remove the debris.

11. Continue rolling over the plants until they are firmly pressed into the clay. Often, especially with bigger pieces, I run the flexible steel scraper over the top of the flattened composition to make sure everything is evenly embedded into the clay and I'm getting as much detail as possible from the plants. Move the scraper very gently over the top—use a combination of angling the scraper a bit and a slight degree of pressure. (Make sure you don't use too much pressure, as you may snag the plant material. Using the scraper at this point isn't essential, but it provides an extra level of detail—it may take some practise.)

12a. Remove each of the plants by carefully lifting them out by the end of their stems, which are positioned outside the frame. Remove as much plant matter as possible from the clay.

12b. Stem segments may leave behind ragged impressions, which is caused by excess clay. You can use a scalpel blade to remove the excess clay and to lift out bits of plants that are stuck in the clay. Be gentle, take your time, and be patient. Because it's quite difficult to hover over the clay without inadvertently making marks, it can be helpful to replace the frame and use it to support the side of your hand as you pick out the plants with the blade. You can also use tweezers, but I use a scalpel blade to remove plants because I find it easier to manipulate, and I also find I'm less likely to damage the detail in the clay inadvertently. Note that the longer you leave plants in the clay, the more difficult it becomes to extricate them—pull out the plant matter as soon as you can.

13. Smear a layer of petroleum jelly on the inside edges of the frame. The wood on a new frame can be relatively porous, so I recommend using plenty of petroleum jelly. This seals the inside edge of the frame before you pour in the plaster and helps make it easier to remove the cast from the frame later.

14. Replace the frame on the clay in a position that you're happy with. Don't worry if you have lost the original outline; it was just an initial guide. Gently hammer the frame. It should sit firmly on the surface and should not be pushed into the clay.

15. Use a flexible steel scraper to cut away some of the excess clay from around the outside of the frame and to create a strip of clay.

16. Place the strip of clay around the outside edges of the frame. Then use your fingers to squidge the clay tight to the frame. This will form a seal that will prevent any plaster leaking out. You can also roll out extra clay into "sausages" and use these to seal the frame edges.

17. Don your face mask to avoid breathing in the fine plaster particles, and then weigh out a suitable amount of plaster powder in a bowl. (See "Measuring the water and plaster" on page 48 for information about how much water and plaster to use.) Pour some water into the flexible mixing bowl. Then start sprinkling the plaster powder into the centre of the bowl of water until it forms a small mound surrounded by a moat of water.

18. Use your hands to mix the plaster and water thoroughly. Aim for a consistency of between half-and-half cream and light whipping cream.

19. Pour the plaster mix into the frame. Always try to pour in one spot, ideally above a place of high detail rather than a blank area. The place where the plaster is poured often ends up looking slightly marbled and less smooth, as the plaster and clay combine slightly. This "pour mark" will be far less obvious if you pour the plaster over an area of the composition that has lots of detail. Note that if you haven't mixed up quite enough plaster to fill the frame, you can mix up more and add it to the frame, so long as the first pour hasn't yet set.

20. Lift up the work board by its edges and gently tap it down a few times on the table to release any air bubbles in the plaster. You need to ensure that no air bubbles are trapped in the plaster (just as you would when making a cake).

21. Use the spirit level to check that the frame and the clay are level. If the clay in the frame isn't level, you can use small, slim bits of wood as chocks under the board to make it perfectly horizontal. The level can be affected by the evenness of your floor or wobbliness of your worktable.

22. Allow the plaster to set for at least an hour.

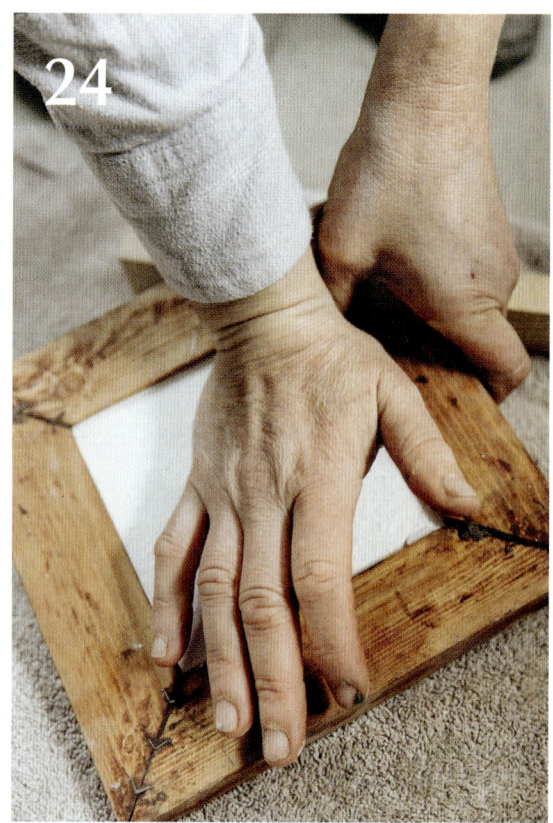

23. Once the plaster has completely set, gently peel the clay away from the back of the frame.

24. At this point, you may find it easier to work on the floor rather than at your table. Take the plaster cast out of the frame. Lay down a towel or a piece of soft cloth to prevent damage to the delicate top surface of the casting as it comes out of the frame. Place the frame on the towel with the clay side facing down, and then position a small piece of wood under the edge of the frame to prop it up. At the corner that's propped up, gently use the heel of your hand to push out the plaster cast, rotating the frame so you're gradually easing out the cast, corner by corner.

25a. Now you have your botanical bas-relief cast in its "raw" state. Let it harden for about twenty-four hours or so before you begin to clean away some of the remaining clay. You can use a kitchen sponge, fine-grade sandpaper, and various sizes of paintbrushes to clean the casting. If it's a small piece, you may find it easier to clean the piece under running water; this is a gentler way of cleaning off the clay and gives you more control.

25b. With a large piece that you can't fit into a sink, place a large bowl of water beside the piece and gently use a sponge and brushes to wipe away the clay.

26. To make the square cast edges crisper, sand down the edges with a sanding block (sandpaper wrapped around a block of wood).

Disguising the pour mark

When you pour plaster onto the clay, it creates a mark that looks a bit like marbling. The pour mark occurs after the plaster is poured on to the surface of the clay and a little bit of the clay gets mixed up with the plaster. It's a good idea to pour the plaster into an area of detail so that the marbling effect will be disguised as much as possible. If you pour on to a blank area, the pour mark is usually very distinct. With terracotta clay, the pour mark is even more visible.

Dealing with leakage

Even after all these years, I still make mistakes. I don't always seal the frame well enough with the clay, and some plaster leaks out. The remedy is to push in a bit more clay where it's leaking, not to worry, and clean it up afterwards when it has set.

Making a signature stamp

I generally add a little imprint with a stamp in the corner of my work to make it recognisably mine. I prefer that my logo be neat and discreet so that it doesn't detract from the actual artwork. For my stamp, I used a small length of round dowel onto which I glued my initials using lettering purchased from a model-making company. You could also use a small object such as a button to make a recognisable mark. I like being consistent with where I position my stamp. If you choose to use a stamp, its placement is entirely up to you.

Clockwise:

Pour the plaster onto the clay in an area with lots of detail to disguise the pour mark.

Here the pour mark is still partly visible in the blank area despite being poured into the area with the most details.

Leaking plaster is easily remedied by pushing more clay around the edge of the frame to improve the seal.

I made a little signature stamp from a short length of dowel onto which I glued plastic letters.

Working with clay

There are lots of different types of clay on the market, so it's always worth experimenting. You can use pretty much any type of clay (apart from air-dry clay) to make a botanical bas-relief, as long as it's smooth; each type can provide a different look to the final pieces. I use grey (also known as modelling clay), earthenware, stoneware, and terracotta clays. I use grey clay most often, as I like the subtle effect it leaves in the plaster. I also really like terracotta clay, but the look it creates is quite different because the colour it imparts on the plaster is richer and more pronounced.

If you use terracotta clay, you can implement the cleaning up process very gently so that it leaves a sort of velvety surface on the plaster cast. The reddish colour of terracotta clay lends itself particularly well to compositions using autumn and winter plants. Because the colour is quite strong, it can be tricky to fit these pieces in easily within a wider range of interior décor as artwork or wall panels. Most people prefer the grey clay because it is more neutral, rather like a black-and-white photo.

When I'm cleaning up my cast pieces, I don't scrub away all the clay. I like to leave some of the clay in the fine detail, which helps emphasise the contrast and gives more depth to the final piece. When you are using either grey or terracotta clay and you wipe the blank areas completely clean, you're left with crisp, white plaster.

Measuring the clay

The quantity of clay you'll need will depend on the size of the frame you use. Here are some suggestions.

- 12 cm (4¾ in.) square frame—900 g (2 lbs.) clay

- 15 cm (6 in.) square frame—1100 g (2½ lbs.) clay

- 25 cm (10 in.) square frame—3300 g (7¼ lbs.) clay

- 40 cm (15¾ in.) square frame—5000 g (11 lbs.) clay

Clay consistency

The consistency of the clay has a big impact on the results of the casting. To get the best impression in the clay, the clay must be neither too wet nor too dry. If the clay is too wet and sticky, the surface and the rolling pin may become messy and the impression of the plants lose definition. If the clay is too dry and hard, the plants will be squished on the surface after rolling and won't make a deep enough imprint.

If the clay is wet and sticky, remove it from the plastic bag and leave it out for a while to air dry. The excess moisture will evaporate over time. The rate of drying depends on your individual circumstances, so it's best to keep checking the clay until it looks and feels right. Ceramicists use plaster blocks to dry out their clay (plaster sucks moisture out of clay at a faster rate), but that may be too much of an investment for beginners. If your clay is too dry, spray it with some water and leave it under a sheet of plastic until the water is absorbed. Again, keep checking until you're happy with the moisture content.

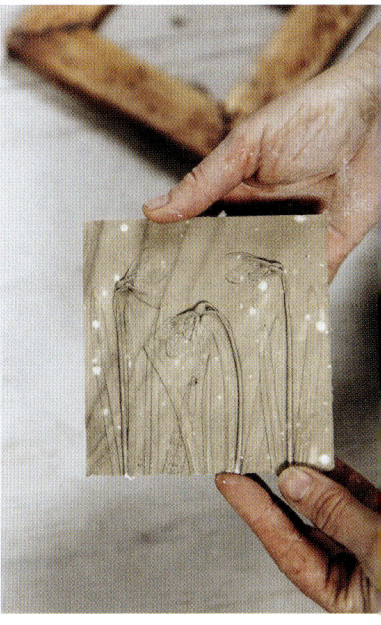

Dimples in the clay are caused by cold temperatures.

Clay and cold temperatures

In winter, it can be very chilly in my studio. The clay and plaster become cold, and this can affect the results of casting. With cold clay, the plaster cast often ends up with little white spots and dimples on the surface. I don't know what's happening at the chemical level, but I assume the cold is somehow affecting the chemical reaction and how the plaster sets. To avoid this, don't work in a room that's too cold. If you're unsure about the temperature in your work space, you can use warm water to mix the plaster and put the clay and plaster somewhere warm before working with it—or just wait for the weather to improve!

Reusing clay

After I've used a piece of clay to make a casting, I reuse it. I keep it rolled out and remove all the bits of plaster and plant material that are left behind. I add clay to fill any holes and a bit of water to rehydrate the clay. Then I cover it all with a sheet of plastic.

After I revisit the clay later, I sometimes find a tiny plant growing from a seed that had been left behind and had germinated. This always brings to mind the time when I was a child and dropped melon seeds down the sink: I was amazed when I found that they'd germinated and were growing out of the sink overflow!

Working with plaster of Paris

I use plaster of Paris (also known as modelling plaster, model plaster, or hard plaster) to cast most of my botanical bas-relief pieces. With many different types of plaster available, the one you choose depends on many factors, including the size of the cast. I'm continually experimenting with plaster; for general-purpose use, however, I recommend a hard plaster of Paris such as the Crystacal R brand.

The hardness/density in plaster is measured in pounds per square inch (psi). This is the pressure that results when 1 pound of force is applied to a unit area of 1 square inch. Crystacal R is 8000 psi. It's not necessary to get hung up on which plaster to use, because as any plaster will work, even builder's plaster. If in doubt, try to use a harder plaster with a higher density, which will better capture the finer details.

Measuring the water and plaster

When I mix plaster, I don't usually weigh out the plaster beforehand. Over the years, I have learned roughly how much water I need depending on the size of the cast that I'm making. The plaster consistency should be similar to between half-and-half cream and light or whipping cream.

For the purposes of this book, I've created a rough guide to the quantities of water and plaster you'll need for each size of cast. Note that these measurements are just a guide. Check the instructions on the bag of plaster for more specific information.

- 12 cm (4¾ in.) square frame—150 ml (5 oz.) water; 340 g (¾ lb.) plaster

- 15 cm (6 in.) square frame—200 ml (6.75 oz.) water; 440 g (1 lb.) plaster

- 25 cm (10 in.) square frame—600 ml (20 oz.) water; 1200 g (2¾ lbs.) plaster

- 40 cm (15¾ in.) square frame—2000 ml (67.5 oz.) water; 2470 g (5½ lbs.) plaster

Allowing the plaster to set

I recommend allowing the plaster to set in the frame for at least an hour before removing it. It's important that the plaster is firmly set. If you attempt to lift it out too soon, it won't be strong enough to come out of the frame in one piece and the details will attach to the clay and break off the plaster. The plaster can

stay longer than an hour in the frame, but if you leave it in the frame for too long, it can become too hard to push out of the frame, and the petroleum jelly will have been absorbed. There is no problem leaving the clay on plaster, without the frame, for longer periods.

Left: Run a scalpel blade along the edge of the cast to remove excess plaster.

Right: Clean the casting with sandpaper.

Tidying up the casting

The plaster often spreads beyond the edges of the frame. I generally tidy this up by running a scalpel along the edges of the plaster. Or you can leave the plaster as is if you like the ragged edges.

After you have removed the clay from the frame and the plaster is completely dry, you may want to remove some of the clay that remains on the surface and in the detail. You can do this by using a sponge, various sized brushes, and various grits of sandpaper. When I use sandpaper to clean a casting, I usually start with 80 grit, then move to finer grit paper—from 120, to 180, and then to 320 grit. Take care when using sandpaper, because there is always a possibility that you may end up rubbing off some of the details.

How much clay you remove or leave in place is a matter of personal taste. You may choose to leave the cast as is, in its raw state, or you could remove all of the clay by scrubbing the cast completely clean. I prefer to leave some of the clay in the detail. Often the impressions made by small, delicate petals can be so subtle that you need to leave traces of the clay to help define the impressions by creating some contrast. It's sort of like how a detective puts powder over latent fingerprints to make them visible; the powder helps increase the contrast that clearly reveals the fingerprints.

Working with Plants and Casting Techniques

4

C hoosing and arranging plants is one of the most enjoyable parts of this process, so make the most of it by taking your time. My garden in London isn't very big, but I try to plant in such a way that I have at least some flowers to enjoy throughout the year. The pieces I create are most often a reflection of what's growing at a particular moment in time, so, as an added bonus, my work provides the perfect opportunity to appreciate what each season has to offer and take a close look at the plants I love.

Working with "squishy" plants

Some plants contain sap, which can be toxic and can cause skin irritation. If you use plants that exude sap when cut or exude liquid when pressed into the clay, wash your hands after handling them and avoid touching your eyes and face. If in doubt, wear protective clothing such as latex gloves and goggles while handling the plants.

Common plants with sap that can cause serious skin irritation include monkshood (*Aconitum* spp.), arum lilies (*Arum* spp.), daphne (*Daphne* spp.), angel's trumpet (*Brugmansia*), spurge (*Euphorbia* spp.), and giant hogweed (*Heracleum mantegazzianum*). You can research plants using various plant finder apps and the internet.

Another issue with squishy plants is that you may inadvertently spread the sap over the clay and make a sticky mess. Plants that are succulent with juicy leaves and stems are often problematic for this reason. You don't always know how plants will respond until you decide to roll over them. Remember to keep wiping the rolling pin with a lint-free cloth, and make sure the surface of clay remains relatively dry by carefully cleaning it with a soft sponge. Be careful when wiping the clay, however, because that can also leave marks. As you continue rolling, these marks will often flatten out under the pressure of the rolling pin.

Choosing and arranging plants

Looking for plants to cast makes me see the garden in a way that I simply wouldn't if I was just appreciating the plants in nature or even taking a snap with a camera. It's more observational, a bit like when I am sketching or drawing. When I cast a collection of the same plant, the process enables me to compare and contrast the subtle differences in detail and invariably makes me want to find out more about a plant's history and origins.

I'm often asked what is my favourite plant, but it's impossible for me to choose. I love all plants! When I'm looking for specimens to cast, however, I'm predominantly searching for those with interesting shapes, habits, textures, or details. In terms of composition, I aim for something airy with some elements of interest overlapping. I like to cast daisy shapes and dangly plant parts. And there's something about a red-hot poker (*Kniphofia* spp.) that reminds me of a 1920s flapper's dress—the way the petals hang down in layers.

Choosing the right plants is the first step to getting a good end result, whether you use a bunch of flowers purchased from a florist or some of your favourites picked from the garden or along a hike. Think about flowers, foliage, and stems and how the various shapes and textures might work together. It may take a few tries to perfect a composition, but that's all part of the process.

The only plants I'd recommend avoiding are what we think of as "classic" roses, especially those stiff Valentine's Day, commercially grown, cut roses, which don't cast well at all and always end up looking like a small fist in the plaster. This is unfortunate, because florists frequently use these types of roses in wedding bouquets. The very old-fashioned garden roses and species roses that have more open forms can create beautiful impressions, however. Also, little spray roses (sometimes called sweetheart roses), which form clusters of small flowers, cast well.

Plants are best picked first thing in the morning when temperatures are cool and everything is nice and fresh. After picking, plunk them in water immediately. After I pick smaller plants, I put them in a glass of water in the fridge to keep them looking good for even longer. With larger plants, keeping them in a bucket of water somewhere shady and cool will keep them fresh. It's also a good idea to keep a record of the plants you use by taking pictures of the casts you make. I find it useful to look back at those images to assess mistakes and successes.

Working with dried plants

Often the beauty of the underlying structure is revealed when plants are dry, and I've had great results when I cast from dried cow parsley (*Anthriscus sylvestris*) and hydrangea seedheads. I've also cast twigs in bud, catkins, and pussy willows (although, to be honest, none of these were completely dried out). But dried plants are difficult to cast. Although many can be used to make beautiful impressions, most are too brittle and leave too many bits behind in the clay. Also, in the process of picking out the little bits that can be very tricky to remove, you can inadvertently destroy the detail that you need to make a good cast.

If you want to cast dried plants, be mindful of what you choose because it can become annoying and time-consuming to pick the seeds and broken parts out of the clay. Grasses, in particular, tend to leave most of their little seedheads behind. That's not to say you shouldn't experiment, but you may find that the process is so laborious that all joy is lost. For acorns and rose hips, which are plump and smooth, I often smear them with a tiny bit of petroleum jelly before pressing them into the clay; this makes them easier to release from the clay and leaves a better impression. If some bits of the plant remain in the clay, it's not the end of the world, and they can actually add something special to the end result. Think of it as a little bit of DNA, a time capsule captured in the plaster for future generations.

Arranging plants

For me, creating a composition is a very unconscious process. I'll play around with an arrangement until it feels right. Overall, I'm looking to create a feeling of movement and space. It's mainly a matter of knowing when enough is enough, and I always have in my head "contrast, contrast, contrast". Traditional botanical drawings show the various aspects of a plant, and I like to do the same with my casts—whether that means showing both sides of a leaf or flower or using specimens that show the transition from bud to flower to seedhead. I tend to use the combination of shapes as my guide. To be honest, there are only so many ways that you can position the plants—horizontally in a row, or undulating either with a peak in the middle and sloping sides or with peaks at either end that slope toward the middle.

Although I have some general rules about arranging the plants, I prefer not to be prescriptive. Experimentation is the best way to learn. The process is like music, because there's a rhythm to it. I play around and arrange the plants into pleasing compositions and invariably try to maintain a hint of the movement the plants would have in the garden or in the wild. I try to make the composition look as naturalistic as possible. I work very intuitively and simply fiddle around until it feels right. Your experience may not feel exactly like mine, because what works for me may not work for you. To a large extent, you really can't go wrong, because plants are so lovely. Nature is the best artist. Bear in mind that the composition doesn't have to be botanically accurate in terms of height or position. I like to think of it more as a flower arrangement, not a replica of the outdoors. Use your instinct, and if it feels right to you, then go for it.

Before placing plants on the clay, play around with them on your work surface or on a board of a similar size to the frame you plan to use. As soon as you place something on the surface of the clay, it will make a bit of an impression. Be careful and work slowly. Position the plants very lightly on the clay and know that once something is pressed in, there's no going back. Also be aware that whenever you squash plant material into the clay, it will lose a bit of its original character. With practise, you will learn how the plants tend to behave when they're rolled into the clay. Also, when placing stems, make sure that they physically extend past the bottom edge of the clay; this makes it easier to grab hold of them and gently lift the plants out of the clay after the impression without marking the clay.

I usually start by positioning the flowers first, and then the foliage. I tend to choose a single stem as the main feature to start off the design, and then I work everything else into the composition from there. It makes sense to begin with a strong, dynamic shape and use that as the catalyst for the rest of the composition. In terms of size, I find it best to let the taller plants set the scene with the

smaller ones coming up like babies around it. I also consider the empty space around and above the plants. With smaller tiles, I aim to fill the frame while still leaving a bit of space around the arrangement. For larger pieces, I tend to leave space at the top of the frame and make sure that some of this space also extends down and between some of the plants.

I rarely position stems bolt upright; placing them at angles makes them look more naturalistic. Always bear in mind how a plant holds itself in nature and use that as a guide. Ideally, the composition will celebrate and exaggerate a plant's intrinsic characteristics. Try to get the best out of the plants you use. If you're including a really beautiful leaf or flower, it doesn't make sense to obscure it behind something else.

When I'm working with flowers, I usually place the head of a flower face first into the clay to get the interior detail impression. If I include a number of the same or very similar plants, I try to make things more interesting and dynamic by giving them a slightly different treatment, such as casting the back, side, and front profiles to make other aspects of the plant viewable. With leaves, I usually place their undersides into the clay to make the impression, because this is where the veins and details are most prominent.

The plants you choose and how you combine them are both important factors, but the way you place the various elements, so that some sit above and others below, also makes a big difference to the final outcome. Layering the plants is a bit like weaving. Once the plants are partially down, I might lift up the odd leaf and slip another leaf underneath just to vary the movement within the piece. Only when I'm happy with the composition do I use the roller to flatten it into place. Be aware that, with repeated rolling, the initial impression made with the frame may be lost. Usually, it's obvious where the frame should go, but at the final stage, you can reposition the frame if you think the composition can be improved.

Considering scale

The size of a piece is invariably dictated by the sizes of the plants. In winter, the plants are often small, but in summer I tend to work on a far bigger scale, not only because plants tend to be taller and fuller in high season but because the garden has a lot more on offer. If working on smaller tiles, I think using one type of plant looks best. I'll often use either a single stem or a group of three plants. I also tend to make sure the frame of a small casting is quite full. With larger casts, I like to leave some empty space around the plants.

Considering colour

Obviously, once the plants are cast, they are colourless and appear as monotone in the final piece. Although I don't consciously arrange the plants with colour in mind, I suspect I do so subconsciously. If you plan to paint a casting, it's definitely worth taking into account how the colours will fit together in an arrangement.

Casting in concrete

I occasionally cast in concrete rather than plaster. Concrete creates a different aesthetic, and has more of an 'industrial' look. Because of the coarse nature of concrete, the end result is not as precise as I achieve when casting in plaster, and the work is not as smooth. Concrete castings can be displayed outside, though I don't always make them specifically to be used outdoors. If you decide to display a concrete bas-relief outdoors, it can be either hung or propped up against a wall, just like an indoor decorative casting. One of the nice things about displaying the work outdoors is that it tends to weather nicely over time; in the rainy weather where I live, my outdoor pieces eventually become covered in beautiful green moss.

Concrete is generally made of cement (the binder), aggregate (gravel, crushed stone, and similar materials), sand, and water. I prefer not to include aggregate in my castings because it creates a texture that is too coarse to capture the plants' details. I use builder's sand. I've also played around with using white marble dust and white cement (instead of regular grey cement) to make a white concrete bas-relief, and the surface texture was pretty much the same as using regular cement and sand.

Be sure to mix the cement, sand, and water really well to get the right consistency. I aim for a consistency that's thicker than cream, more along the lines of a cake mix, that flows fairly easily. When it comes to pouring the concrete onto the clay, unlike plaster, it doesn't leave a pour mark. Still, I always pour in one place, usually a corner, and avoid moving it around. Concrete also takes a lot longer to set than plaster, and I leave it for five to seven days before removing the clay.

The trickiest part of casting in concrete is that the clay can be difficult to remove. Because the concrete can take up to a week to set, the clay tends to dry out and becomes leathery. Removing it is a bit like an archaeologist's dig—you have to chip off the clay bit by bit. When cleaning up the final piece, it's a matter of scrubbing gently and making sure you don't scrub away too much detail in the process.

Measuring the concrete mix

When I cast in concrete, I use a standard mix of four parts sand to one part cement. I prefer a coarse sand known as sharp sand, grit sand, rough sand, or concreting sand. The final consistency should be sort of sloppy, like porridge. The following examples are approximate guidelines.

- 40 cm (15¾ in.) square piece—10 cups sand and 2½ cups cement, or 3750 g (8¼ lbs.) sand and 650 g (1½ lbs.) cement; 1 cup water

- 25 cm (10 in.) square piece—4 cups sand and 1 cup cement, or 1270 g (2¾ lbs.) sand and 250 g (½ lbs.) cement; ½ cup water

Instructions

1. Make the concrete mix using four parts sand to one part cement, then add water slowly until it reaches a sloppy, porridge-like consistency.

2. Pour the mix into your frame as you would plaster, taking care that your board is level and the mix spreads evenly over the surface.

3. I usally leave the concrete to set thoroughly for 5-7 days before removing the clay and cleaning the piece up. As the clay is drier and harder, it's a case of carefully chipping it off bit by bit.

4. Casts made in concrete have a coarser, more industrial look and, unlike plaster, can be displayed outdoors.

Making a silicone mould

If you're interested in making numerous botanical bas-relief castings from one composition, you can use a silicone mould to make multiple copies of the same design in plaster or other materials. You can also play around with colour variations in different pieces. Plaster or concrete capture the detail in the silicone mould in much the same way that they do in the clay when you're making a direct one-off casting.

Although various options for mould making are available, silicone is the most effective one, but silicone mixes can be expensive. Several types of silicone are available, and all are equally effective. Moulds can be complicated, but this single-piece mould is about as simple and straightforward as you can get.

If you purchase a silicone moulding mix kit, it will include instructions about how to prepare the material. I recommend you follow them precisely. Included in the kit will be a catalyst, which helps the silicone cure at room temperature and usually comes in various colours. I much prefer using a coloured catalyst to the clear variety, because when mixing it with the white silicone, I can judge whether or not I've mixed everything together properly.

Before adding the catalyst, I suggest you give the bottle a really good shake. I once made the mistake of trying to create a silicone mould after I didn't mix up the catalyst properly. The consistency seemed fine and the colour was very red, but the whole mix never set, and it ended up like sticky chewing gum. It took a lot of hard work to clean it off the plaster!

When determining how much silicone mix you should use to make the mould, think about the quantity of plaster you used when making the original plaster cast as a guide. I suggest you write it down when you create the plaster cast so you don't forget. You'll use the same amount of silicone mix, plus an additional 25 percent. So, for example, if you used 340 g (0.75 lb.) of plaster for the cast, you'd need to use about 450 g (1 lb.) of silicone mix. As you're working, if you find that you haven't created enough silicone for the mould, you can simply make more and add it immediately, or even after it's set. Ideally, the silicone should cover about 3 mm (⅛ in.) or so above the highest point of the plaster cast.

A silicone mould can last for several years before it falls apart, though this depends on the number of times you cast into it. Each cast using a mould is called a pull. I've never actually counted how many pulls I've made from each mould. I tend to keep the master plaster cast so that I can make another silicone mould if needed.

Materials

- cardboard box (such as a pizza box) with a depth of at least 5 cm (2 in.)

- scissors or craft knife

- packaging tape (packing tape)

- stiff, flat board (wider than the box)

- plaster cast

- spirit (bubble) level

- plastic mixing tub

- wooden spoon

- silicone moulding mix and catalyst

Instructions

1. Prepare the container that will hold the silicone mixture. For the purposes of this mould, a pizza box is the perfect size. Cut off the lid, and then use packaging tape to seal up holes in the base and the gaps around the sides, paying particular attention to where the corners are folded in. The aim is to make it leakproof. The box should be at least 5 cm (2 in.) larger than the cast you'll use for the mould.

2. Place the box on the work board, and then put the plaster cast in the centre of the box. Leave an even amount of space around the cast.

3. Use a spirit level to check that the box is level on the work surface or table.

4. In the plastic tub, use a wooden spoon to mix the silicone and catalyst according to the instructions. Make sure to mix the two components together very well. The silicone pictured here is white and the catalyst is red.

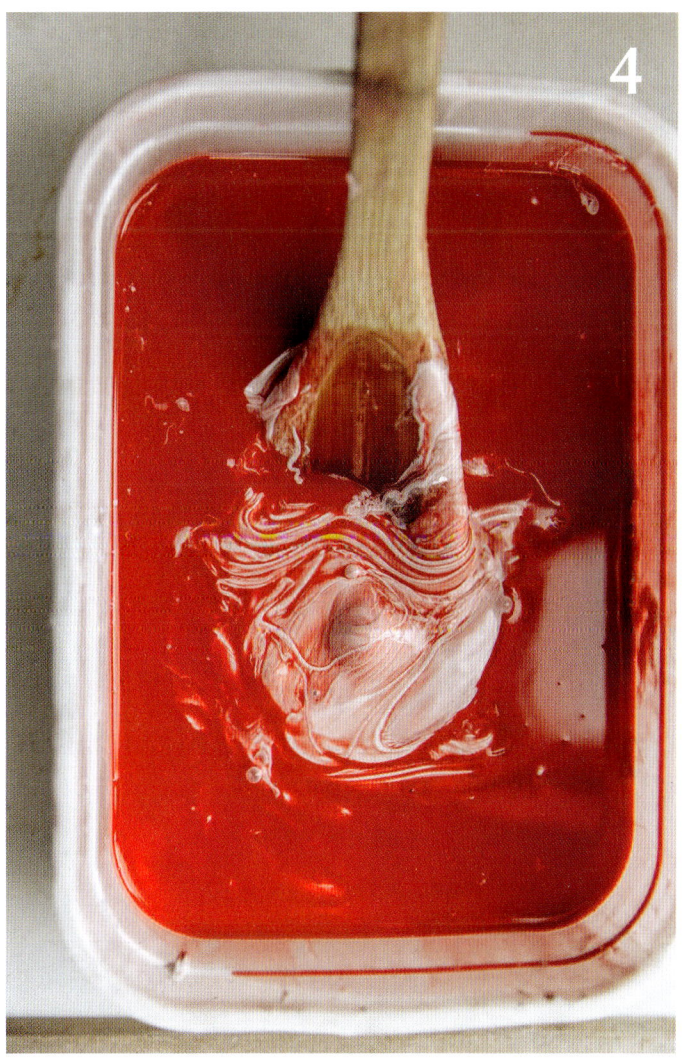

5. Pour the silicone mix over the plaster cast starting at the middle, and then leave it to set. The silicone mix quickly settles and finds its own level. Make sure that the silicone covers everything, ideally to a depth of at least 3 mm (⅛ in.). Air bubbles may arise, but they will pop without your help. Don't move the mould for at least twenty-four hours to allow it to set thoroughly.

6. Once the silicone is set, cut it away from the cardboard box using scissors or a knife. The silicone may leak beneath the base of the cast, so you may need to cut off the overspill. You need to be fairly firm when cutting; don't worry about cutting into the plaster because the silicone is on the back side of the cast.

7. Peel the silicone mould off the plaster cast.

Creating a colourful bas-relief

I really love colour, and I'm particularly interested in the colour of the flowers I'm working with. I often struggle with the concept of adding colour to a bas-relief because I think the work seems more authentic when it's left in its original, uncoloured state.

When I choose to add pigment to the plaster when using a silicone mould, I like to play around with different colours. I encourage you to be experimental. When mixing pigments into plaster, you have to work fast so that the plaster doesn't set before you finish mixing, and you never know exactly what you're going to end up with. Sometime the results can be quite surprising!

Painting a finished bas-relief with watercolours, on the other hand, is more predictable. You can apply the paint slowly and it seeps into the plaster, like a stain. If you make a mistake with watercolour, to some extent (if you're quick) you can scrape it off carefully with a knife blade.

Use watercolour paints and a variety of different sized paintbrushes and take your time to build up the colours gradually.

Using watercolours

I've had a lot of fun playing around with adding colour to my plaster casts. I use a set of watercolours from Winsor & Newton that I've had since childhood. At art college, I was taught never to use the paint straight out of the pot, but rather to mix the colour myself and test it out on the palette. For me, doing this makes the colours far more interesting and gives the piece a much more natural look.

As I paint, I'm careful not to overdo the colour and lose the natural look. Although I have tried gouache (which is opaque), I prefer the more subtle effect I can get using watercolours. The plaster draws in the colour of the watercolour paints, which helps bring out the detail. Rather than a thick layer of paint on top of the cast, watercolours offer lightness and subtlety, and you can play around with accentuating the veins, crevices, and outlines of the plants.

It's not necessary to prepare the plaster cast before painting. Simply load a paintbrush with watercolour paint and gradually build up the layers over the dry plaster. I use a palette to mix the colours along with two pots of water. I use the water to clean the brushes as I work: one pot ends up with a lot of pigment in it, and the other is relatively clean so that I can dip the brush in it to keep it as clean as possible between applications of paint. I use a range of different sized brushes, including some very fine ones, because some of the work is very delicate (stems, for example, can be particularly narrow).

If the paint bleeds into unintended areas, you can use a scalpel blade to gently scrape away the colour (however, it doesn't remove everything). With stems, the paint tends to get drawn down into the outlining edge, which doesn't always look very naturalistic. Because the process of making a botanical bas-relief is relatively cheap and quick, you don't need to be too precious. You can try to scrub away any mistakes, but if that doesn't work, take another look: you may have inadvertently created something interesting. If you do mess up, don't fret! Just embrace it as part of the learning curve.

I have mixed feelings about using colour on my botanical bas-reliefs. Sometimes I think, "Oh no, this is too bright, too twee, too chocolate-boxy." But on the other hand, I do like the process of painting, and the results can be really pretty. Overall, I think I prefer leaving the plaster plain, but I encourage you to experiment and find your own style.

Adding colour pigment to plaster

You can use artist's pigments to add colour to the plaster (or concrete) before you pour it onto the clay or silicone mould. These are usually available in a powdered form and can be purchased from an artist supply shop. I never use the pigment straight out of the pot. I may add a tiny bit of black to a blue pigment, or perhaps a bit of green and a bit of red.

Blue and green pigments are among the most expensive colours, whereas the more natural and earthy colours, such as ochre, ombre, and terracotta (which I favour), are more economical. I have experimented with liquid pigments used for resin, but these tend to be very bright and intense, which isn't a look I want to pursue.

As you add pigment, keep in mind that the light-coloured plaster dilutes the colour considerably. You'll need to use a lot of pigment to get a decent depth of colour. It's also difficult to get a flat, even colour. And darker pigment colours tend to create more uneven end results. Here's how to add pigment to plaster for a single-colour cast.

Materials

- rubber gloves
- mask
- glass bowl
- pigment
- pestle or mortar and pestle
- water
- plaster of Paris
- mixing bowl
- spatula
- prepared clay or silicone mould
- frame
- sieve (optional)

Instructions

1. Put on rubber gloves and a mask.

2. In a glass bowl, add a few heaping teaspoons of pigment. How much pigment you add depends on how intense you would like the colour to be—the more pigment you add, the more intense the colour becomes. So, for instance, add three heaped teaspoons of blue pigment and half a teaspoon of black pigment to the bowl.

3. Use a pestle (or mortar and pestle) to grind the pigment to a fine powder. Add a few tablespoons of water along with a couple teaspoons of plaster to make a thickish paste. (The consistency is not really important—adding water is just a way to facilitate the process of grinding.) Remember that plaster sets within about twenty minutes, so you'll need to work quickly.

4. Using a spatula, mix up a bowl of plaster (quantity depending on the size of your cast). Then incrementally mix the ground pigment/plaster mixture into the plaster. Keep stirring and adding pigment mixture until you're happy with the colour.

5. Scrape the plaster/colour mix out of the bowl and into the frame with the clay or silicone mould. I sometimes use a sieve as I pour to make sure there are no lumps in the plaster.

Many different colours can be used for Wedgwood-style castings.

How to make a bas-relief in the style of Wedgwood

When I first started casting in silicone moulds, I was initially disappointed with the details produced compared to those of my original bas-reliefs and put it aside. But I persevered and started to play around with adding colour. As soon as I tried putting white plaster into the detail with a coloured background, bingo! The first bas-relief I made in this style included a row of white snowdrops against a pale blue background. The details really stood out, and I loved the effect. I also experimented with using black details against a white background, which looked quite gothic. I've since used various colours for the background and the detail. These days, I like to use white plaster for the details and coloured plaster for the background, but you could put darker colours into the detail, though darker shades do tend to bleed.

The materials used to make this cast are similar to those used in other casts. Here's how to make a bas-relief with white detail and a blue background.

Instructions

1. Place the silicone mould on a strong, flat board. Make sure it is level.

2. Put on rubber gloves and a mask.

3. In a small bowl, mix up a small amount of plaster of Paris.

4. Add a bit of plaster to the silicone mould and use your fingers to push the plaster into the details. Pouring plaster into the silicone mould is different from pouring it onto clay because the silicone is flexible—a bit like an ice-cube container—and has an oily surface that tends to resist the plaster, so you need to work the plaster into all the cavities to avoid air bubbles forming.

5. Once you've filled in the detail with plaster, lift up the mould and gently tap it down on the work surface (as you would a cake tin) to release any trapped air bubbles.

6. Drag a flexible steel scraper across the surface to remove excess plaster. The plaster should remain only in the areas of detail.

7. Allow the plaster to set in the mould for forty-five minutes to two hours. Do not allow it to set for much longer than that, because the plaster can start to ping out of the mould. Conversely, if you move on to the next step too soon, the white plaster can mix with the coloured plaster that you pour in next. You'll want the details in the plants to stay crisp and well-defined.

8. Use a mortar and pestle (or a glass bowl and pestle) to grind up the pigment to a fine powder. You can use a single colour from the pot or mix a couple of pigments together to make the colour more interesting and unique. I use a natural blue pigment with a tiny bit of black to create this look. Even with just two pigments, you can get a huge variety of colours by altering the quantities of each. Be aware that the amount of plaster that you add subsequently will change the intensity of the colour.

9. Add a little bit of plaster and water to the ground pigment to make a paste. Then set it aside.

10. Working quickly, make up some plaster in a flexible mixing bowl. The amount you'll need to make depends on the size of your mould.

11. Using a spatula, add the coloured paste to the bowl of plaster. The consistency of the mix should be between half-and-half cream and light whipping cream. Keep in mind that when the plaster is fully dried, the colour will be much lighter than when you're mixing it.

12. Pour the plaster mix into the silicone mould. Then gently tap it on the work surface to release any air bubbles. Set it aside on a flat surface.

13. Allow it to set for at least two hours. The cast needs to be fairly robust to release easily from the silicone mould.

14a. Pull the cast out of the mould.

14b. Set the cast aside to dry. When the cast comes out of the mould, the colour may look a bit patchy, but it usually evens out as it dries. I sometimes sand the surface of the cast to make the colour more even, but this technique is not always successful.

14a

Hanging your bas-relief

I like a simple, pared-back aesthetic and create my botanical bas-reliefs in such a way that they can be hung flush against a wall without a frame. To make them self-supporting, I make sure the casts are relatively deep so I can drill either a single hole or attach a mirror plate from which I can hang them. You could attach a cord to the back of the bas-relief and hang it from that, but the cast will tip forward from the wall (and, personally, I'm not keen on that).

Single-hole hanger

Often, I find the simplest methods are the best. Although a single-hole hanger is not necessarily the most secure method of hanging a bas-relief, I have pieces that have been on my wall for fourteen years, and they've not fallen off yet! I'm always mindful, however, not to hang the pieces where they may unintentionally get knocked off the wall. If you live somewhere prone to earthquakes, I'd suggest you use a slotted mirror plate to hang your bas-relief instead of a single-hole hanger.

I purposely cast my smaller pieces a bit chunkier to ensure that there is more than enough plaster to drill into safely. I find it's better to err on the side of caution. Plus, thicker pieces are more robust when pushed out of the frame. I'm also consistent with the positioning of the holes and hanging fixtures in my casts so that all the pieces I make will hang in the same manner. I generally position the hole around one-third of the way down from the top of the tile and at the horizontal centre of the tile.

With a small, relatively lightweight plaster cast, you can simply drill a hole in the back so that a screw or nail fixed into the wall can be slotted into it.

Materials

- bas-relief cast or tile
- ruler
- pencil
- drill
- drill bit
- tape

Instructions

1. Measure across the width of the piece to find the centre, and mark it with a pencil.

2. Measure one-third of the way from the top of the tile and mark it with a pencil.

3. Every cast you make will be subtly different in depth, and you don't want to drill the hole too deep or you'll drill completely through the plaster. To avoid this, measure the depth of the cast, and then wrap a bit of tape around the drill bit at the point at which you need to stop drilling as a guide. So, for example, if the cast is 14 mm (about ½ in.) deep, you'll need to drill about 10 mm (about ⅓ in.) into the back.

4. Holding the drill at a right angle, drill down into the back of the cast as far as the tape on the drill bit. Make sure you don't drill completely through the plaster.

Place the bent wire hook in the back of the wet-piece concrete.

Wire hook in concrete

When I cast a botanical bas-relief in concrete, I use a short length of wire that I twist and bend and embed in the back of the piece before the concrete sets. The wire is shaped like a curly *W* with a twist to form a loop in the middle. I position the hook in the horizontal centre and one-quarter of the way down the casting. Note that it can be tricky to be precise, because you can't mark the wet concrete, so you have to do it by eye. But not to worry, because if the wire is not completely centred, you can bend it after the concrete is set.

Slotted mirror plate

For bigger pieces, I recommend using a slotted mirror plate, which is a more secure way to hang a heavy casting. The mirror plate is a metal fitting with a keyhole-shaped slot cut into it, which fits over a screw head to lock it into place on the wall. Mirror plates come in several sizes; the size of the plate you'll need depends on the size of the piece. (For example, for a 40 cm [15¾ in.] square piece, I use a 5 cm [2 in.] mirror plate. For a 25 cm [10 in.] square piece, I use a 3 cm [about 1¼ in.] mirror plate.)

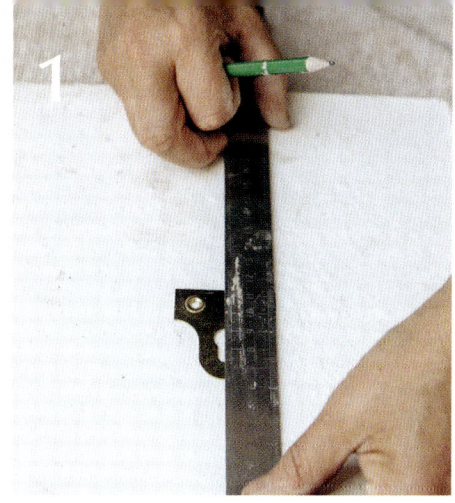

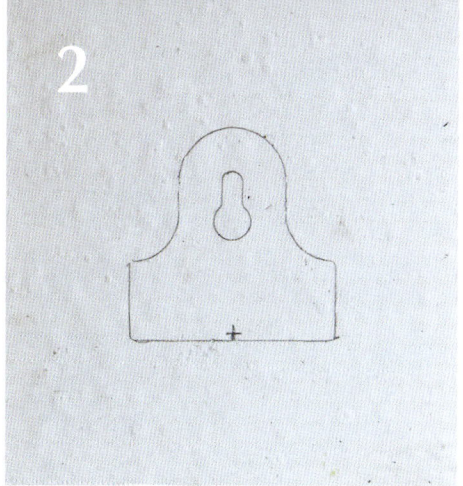

Instructions

1. Measure midway across the back of the cast and about one-third of the way down from the top. Position the mirror plate at that spot.

2. Trace around the plate and the keyhole slot with a pencil. Then place the mirror plate to the side.

3. Drill an oversized hole in the back of the cast at the top of the marked keyhole slot, where the slot will fit over a screw. The size of the drill bit used will depend on the size of the mirror plate. Add a bit of tape to mark the drill bit to indicate how deep you can drill down, and make sure you don't drill completely through the plaster.

4. Score the area within the outline of the mirror plate with a knife to rough it up. This will create a better surface for the glue to adhere to.

5. Glue the plate into position with two-part epoxy glue and allow it to set for at least thirty minutes.

Botanical Bas-Relief in Every Season

5

The scale of each piece I create is a direct response to the size of the plants I'm using. In winter, I tend to concentrate on small, more intimate compositions, while in summer the wider range of plants and more substantial, exuberant growth means my pieces can be bigger and more elaborate. My own relatively small London garden is my main source for plants, but I also use plants grown by friends and occasionally will buy from flower markets and florists. Nature is also a wonderful source of plant material, and I encourage everyone to explore the countryside with a pair of secateurs and some form of carrier. Just be mindful that you don't take anything rare, endangered, or protected, and don't take plants from private gardens without permission.

Wherever you live in the world, take the time to have a good look around you to see what's growing both in the garden and in wilder places. Even the edges of the city can offer interesting plants, and gathering them is a great way to appreciate the changing seasons and what each has to offer. Seeking out and choosing plants that you love are important parts of the whole process.

Compositions for Early Spring

You can tell the season is shifting into early spring by the little pops of colour and the general feeling of profusion of new life that suddenly arrives in the garden. I like spring for its lovely freshness and the way things appear in neat little bunches, almost as if by design. There's a certain sweetness and purity to the plants at this time of year. Generally, most plants are still relatively diminutive in size and lend themselves to smaller castings, similar to those I produce in wintertime.

The finished piece with much
of the terracotta clay left on
the surface

Grape hyacinths

- 15 cm (6 in.) square

- terracotta clay, plaster

- grape hyacinth (*Muscari* spp.)

Grape hyacinth is one of the first flowers I ever cast. These diminutive flowering bulbs are often sweetly scented and can happily self-seed in the right conditions. They have a lovely sculptural quality, and their small, bobbly flower spikes, made up of numerous tiny bells, cast particularly well.

This arrangement uses seven stems of hyacinth arranged so that they splay out slightly from the centre, as they would when growing naturally. The leaves, like those of snowdrops, separate from the stems when you pick them, so count how many leaves each stem would normally have and add those in your composition. Try placing the flowers down first and then the foliage, weaving the various elements through.

The stems are very juicy (as are bluebells) and exude quite a lot of sap when you roll them into the clay. Take care to keep the rolling pin clean by wiping it down with a lint-free cloth. If you end up with sap on the clay, carefully use a sponge to remove it; otherwise, it can end up being visible in the casting. As you remove the plants from the clay, the majority of the plant will lift out neatly in one piece; however, a few particles may remain. Remove as many particles as you can with the tip of a scalpel blade, taking care not to damage the clay.

Instructions

1. Arrange the stems until you are happy with the layout.

2. Use a rolling pin to flatten the flowers into the clay.

3. Carefully lift the stems to pull the plants out of the clay.

4. Use the tip of a scalpel blade to remove any bits of plant material left in the clay.

5. After the plaster has set, peel off the terracotta clay to reveal the bas-relief.

With the background cleaned,
the remaining grey clay helps
outline the details.

Mixed flowers

- 25 cm (10 in.) square

- grey clay, plaster

- barrenwort (*Epimedium* spp.)

- comfrey (*Symphytum officinale*)

- dog's tooth violet (*Erythronium* 'Pagoda')

- grape hyacinth (*Muscari* spp.)

- oriental poppy (*Papaver orientale*) leaf

- primrose (*Primula* spp.)

- snake's head fritillary (*Fritillaria meleagris*)

- snowflake (*Leucojum* spp.)

- Spanish bluebell (*Hyacinthoides hispanica*)

This medium-sized piece is a snapshot of the spring flowers growing in my garden and is full of pretty, fresh new growth. I added the oriental poppy leaf because the plant had started to emerge in the garden and I like the way the foliage casts. You can clearly see how squashy the grape hyacinth is in this bas-relief.

I positioned the fritillaries as my main feature plants, and then used them as the basis for the rest of the design. I let their leaves settle themselves on the clay naturally, and then directed them a little bit to make a better layout. I particularly like the comfrey, which is a bit pinkish and doesn't grow too big. It always reminds me of a beaded necklace. I think it works really well with the fritillary. The plants nicely fill the square frame and all are placed at similar heights. Although I'm far from a minimalist, I endeavoured not to overcrowd this design, making sure that there were enough spaces between the plants.

Lifting them out of the clay was straightforward, and I managed to get pretty much everything out apart from a bit of pollen on the fritillary. Removing plant matter is really just a matter of having patience and a steady hand.

Instructions

1. Once the clay is rolled flat, position the frame and gently hammer it in place to leave an impression on the surface.

2. Position the plants to create a pleasing design.

3. Press the plants into the clay after being flattened with a rolling pin.

4. Position the frame back into place using the outline made by hammering it in.

5. Once the plaster has set, peel back the clay.

3

4

5

Large mixed flowers

- 40 cm (15¾ in.) square

- grey clay, concrete

- barberry (*Berberis* spp.)

- barrenwort (*Epimedium* spp.)

- blackcurrant (*Ribes nigrum*)

- forget-me-not (*Myosotis* spp.)

- Grecian windflower (*Anemone blanda*)

- honesty (*Lunaria annua*)

- lungwort (*Pulmonaria* spp.)

- primrose (*Primula* spp.)

- snake's head fritillary (*Fritillaria meleagris*)

- Spanish bluebell (*Hyacinthoides hispanica*)

- spurge (*Euphorbia* spp.)

- tulip (*Tulipa* spp.)

- Welsh poppy (*Papaver cambricum*) leaf

- wood sorrel (*Oxalis* spp.)

For this composition, I placed the plants in an undulating form, starting high with the blackcurrant, going lower with the primrose, and then back high again to the bluebell, with a good amount of space at the top and in the centre of the piece. Most plants do undulate in height when growing naturally, and sometimes when using more plants I like to include a bit more space.

Up until recently, I thought that forget-me-nots didn't show up that well when cast, but in fact they do, and I love the way their little seedheads curl up and how the leaves are nice and bristly. I also included blackcurrant (which has a strange smell), barberry, some lilac-coloured Spanish bluebells, a lungwort with a dotty leaf, a yellow barrenwort, primrose, a little blue wood sorrell, wood sorrel, honesty, frittilary, barrenwort leaves, spurge, and a little tulip. Once

pressed into the clay, a tulip will flatten a great deal and often ends up looking almost unrecognisable from the original flower. For this bas-relief, I chose a pointy petaled tulip that held its shape really well.

For larger scale botanical bas-relief pieces such as this design, I often use a longer rolling pin that's wide enough to fit entirely across the clay. I found such a rolling pin in a dumpster—although technically it's not a rolling pin, just a long, cylindrical piece of wood. You can find similar varieties at hardware stores or make something yourself out of a decent sized pole. Rolling plants in bigger pieces isn't much different from rolling plants in smaller works. I used the bigger rolling pin to start off, and then finished with a smaller one.

When lifting the plants out, I found that the bluebell tended to split and didn't necessarily come out cleanly in one go; the blackcurrent and barrenwort

This large concrete botanical bas-relief features a mix of flowers in an undulating layout.

also left debris behind. When you're removing bits lodged in the clay, it's helpful if you can be patient and careful, and don't give up. Often, it's worth picking up any remaining pieces at the point closest to the stem, where it's usually strongest, rather than toward the outer edge. In this instance, I left some of the finer petals in place because I was concerned that I'd make more of a mess of the clay if I took them out.

Instructions

1. After the clay has been rolled flat, position the plants.

2. After pressing the plants into the clay, place the frame over the composition to see how the plants will fit within the outline of the frame.

3. Remove the plant matter by pulling out the stems, and then use a scalpel blade to lift out any remaining bits.

Other suggestions for early spring

These plants can also be used for early spring bas-reliefs.

- crocus (*Crocus* spp.)
- clematis (*Clematis* spp.)
- hazel (*Corylus avellana*) catkins
- hyacinth (*Hyacinthus* spp.)
- netted iris (*Iris reticulata*)
- pasqueflower (*Pulsatilla* spp.)
- periwinkle (*Vinca* spp.)
- species tulip (such as *Tulipa sprengeri*)
- spindle (*Euonymus* spp.)
- viburnum (*Viburnum* spp.)
- violet (*Viola* spp.)
- wallflower (*Erysimum cheiri*)
- willow (*Salix* spp.)
- winter hazel (*Corylopsis* spp.)

Compositions for Late Spring

In late spring, plants are really coming up, with the pretty frothiness of cow parsley and all the bluebells. Everything looks lovely and fresh, but as the days lengthen and temperatures gradually begin to rise, you can tell that summer is just around the corner. Gradually, there seems to be many more plants growing in the garden and lots of useful edible things in the wild, such as wild garlic (ramsons), dandelions, and nettles. Be aware that many of these spring flowers are crunchy and full of sap, so be mindful to keep the clay and rolling pin as clean as possible by carefully wiping each time you roll over the plants.

Most of the grey clay has been
cleaned off, leaving just a
little to emphasize the detail
of the plant.

Wild garlic

- **12 cm (4¾ in.) square**
- **grey clay, plaster**
- **wild garlic (*Allium ursinum*)**

In this composition, I wanted to show the three stages of growth of wild garlic as it transforms from bud to flower. I worked with quite small specimens that had lovely, fresh leaves. I placed them at slight angles so that they gently curve over, as the stems didn't look natural standing bolt upright. In retrospect, perhaps a long and narrow tile may have better suited this composition. Alternatively, it could have been cast as a tryptic, with each tile showing a different growth stage of the plant.

Wild garlic produces a fair amount of squishy sap when you flatten it into the clay, so it's important to keep the rolling pin clean by wiping it frequently with a lint-free cloth. If any of the sap squidges onto the clay, use a soft sponge to remove it. Also, the stem is quite crispy and tends to break when you try to pull it out in one go, so work as slowly and as carefully as possible.

Instructions

1. Position the wild garlic at a slight angle within the outline created by the frame.

2. A flexible steel scraper is helpful for making sure the plant is well and truly pressed into the clay so that you can capture as much of the detail as possible.

3. After repositioning the frame, press the clay around the edges of it to create a seal.

4. The moment when the clay is removed to reveal the bas-relief is exciting.

Opposite: The cast of mixed
wildflowers before and
after being painted with
watercolours

The initial piece with the
background thoroughly
cleaned and some grey clay
left in the detail. (*top*) The
same piece after it had been
painted with watercolours.
(*bottom*)

Mixed wildflowers

- **25 cm (10 in.) square**
- **grey clay, plaster**
- **bluebell (*Hyacinthoides* spp.)**
- **burnet (*Sanguisorba* spp.)**
- **buttercup (*Ranunculus acris*)**
- **clover (*Trifolium* spp.)**
- **cow parsley (*Anthriscus sylvestris*)**
- **dandelion (*Taraxacum officinale*) seedhead**
- **ox-eye daisy (*Leucanthemum vulgare*)**
- **plantain (*Plantago lanceolata*)**
- **red campion (*Silene dioica*)**
- **sticky willy/cleavers (*Galium aparine*)**
- **vetch (*Vicia sativa*)**
- **yarrow (*Achillea* spp.)**

I particularly love spotting wild plants that I know have been bred over years
into cultivars with fancier colours and forms. I find it fascinating that these
are the original forms of ornamental plants we now find in gardens. This cast
includes wild things I found growing locally. When working with sticky willy,
I like that I can really see the texture of it in the casting, and the leaf structure
is interesting too. Be mindful that the plant is quite brittle and breaks easily.
Yarrow also casts really well, although it wilts relatively quickly after picking, so
be sure to use it as soon as possible after harvesting.

This composition is quite straightforward, with all the plants in a row at
similar heights. I left a space of 5 cm (2 in.) at the top. I placed the ox-eye daisies
and buttercups face down to capture the intricate beauty of the interior structure and made sure to leave some areas of empty space between these and the
other plants.

Once everything was in place, I smoothed over the composition with a flexible steel scraper and released a couple of air bubbles by piercing them with a scalpel blade. Lifting out the various elements was relatively straightforward apart from the cow parsley, which left behind a lot of petals in the clay. I did my best to remove them but wasn't too fanatical about it.

Instructions

1. Once you're happy with how the arranged plants look, use your fingertips to nudge them gently into position in the clay.

2. After using the rolling pin, go over the composition with a flexible steel scraper to embed the flowers into the clay and get the best impression.

3. Carefully pierce any air bubbles with a scalpel blade, and then smooth the clay.

4. Peel off the clay, then gently ease the casting out of the frame.

Mixed spring flowers

- 40 cm (15¾ in.) square

- grey clay, plaster

- bleeding-heart (*Lamprocapnos spectabilis,* syn. *Dicentra spectabilis*)

- columbine (*Aquilegia* spp.)

- cranesbill (*Geranium phaeum*)

- fern (*Matteuccia* spp.) fiddleheads

- foamflower (*Tiarella* spp.)

- forget-me-not (*Myosotis sylvatica*)

- fringe cups (*Tellima grandiflora*)

- lilac (*Syringa vulgaris*)

- ornamental onion (*Allium* spp.)

- pasqueflower (*Pulsatilla vulgaris*) seedhead

- Solomon's seal (*Polygonatum × hybridum*)

- Spanish bluebell (*Hyacinthoides hispanica*)

- Welsh poppy (*Papaver cambricum*)

This composition is packed with plants that I intermingled and layered together, leaving just a small amount of empty space in front of the bleeding-heart. These plants all grow in my garden in late spring, and this casting includes those that I absolutely love. I used the bleeding-heart as my "hero" plant because it's really fresh, with pretty heart-shaped flowers that dangle beneath a gently curving stem. I positioned it in the middle of the composition and then worked the rest of the design around it.

The columbine is quite a simple flower, which I prefer to the more elaborate, highly bred types, and it hangs the way it would naturally, with the flower pointing downward. It has a good leaf shape, too. I also like Solomon's seal, particularly when the plants are quite small, as well as the fringe cups, which

form sweet little pyramids of flowers. Ferns are such timeless plants and always make lovely impressions, though they do tend to leave bits behind in the clay, especially near the bottom of the stem. The Welsh poppy has very fine petals, and parts of it can be quite challenging to remove from the clay. Nevertheless, it was relatively straightforward to remove the majority of the plants from the clay, and I was able to remove much of the bits that remained behind. Even though sometimes it's fiddly to do so, paying attention to these details often makes a difference in the end result.

The finished piece with the surface cleaned

1. This large composition includes lots of spring plants.

2. Once the plants are rolled and smoothed into the clay, the frame can be repositioned.

1. It can take time to remove little bits remaining in the clay, but it's worth the effort.

2. After the clay is peeled off, the finished composition is revealed.

Other suggestions for spring compositions

These plants are also lovely in a spring bas-relief.

- cherry (*Prunus* spp.) blossoms

- Himalayan clematis (*Clematis montana*)

- honesty (*Lunaria* spp.)

- magnolia (*Magnolia* spp.)

- ostrich fern (*Matteuccia struthiopteris* spp.) fiddleheads

- primrose (*Primula* spp.)

- stachyurus (*Stachyurus* spp.)

- sweet pea (*Lathyrus vernus*)

- wood anemone (*Anemone nemorosa*)

Compositions for Early Summer

I really love summer! Overall, I think it's the feeling of true abundance that I love most. Plants are generally taller, bigger, and more sprawling, and where I live things are still green and lush. Summer provides a great array of colours, including wonderfully bright and clashing hues. The summer landscape also includes a wider variety of shapes and forms to explore compared to other seasons. This means I have the potential to create something bigger and more substantial.

Cosmos and feverfew

- 12 cm (4¾ in.) square

- grey clay, plaster

- cosmos (*Cosmos* spp.)

- feverfew (*Tanacetum parthenium*)

With this bas-relief tile, I wanted to demonstrate how you can treat a layout more like a pattern. I also knew that this was something I wanted to paint, so I had that in mind as I worked. I really like the contrast of the white edge of the casting alongside the painted area.

The cosmos and feverfew flowers are both daisy shapes, but I think there is a good dynamic between the flowers' sizes. I placed all the flowers face down with their petals splayed out. It was quite fiddly, as they are made up of lots of tiny petals. I have used feverfew in other pieces, placing the back of the flowers against the clay, and this makes a lovely striped effect. Fine petals often leave quite subtle impressions, so the way you clean up the work can make a huge difference in the final bas-relief. Generally, I leave traces of clay around the plants to emphasise their shapes.

There's something quite sweet about making patterns with plants on a small scale.

Instructions

1. Cosmos and feverfew flowers are arranged here so that they filled up the entire frame.

2. After pulling out the plants, a few stamens and petals may remain, but they can be easy to extricate.

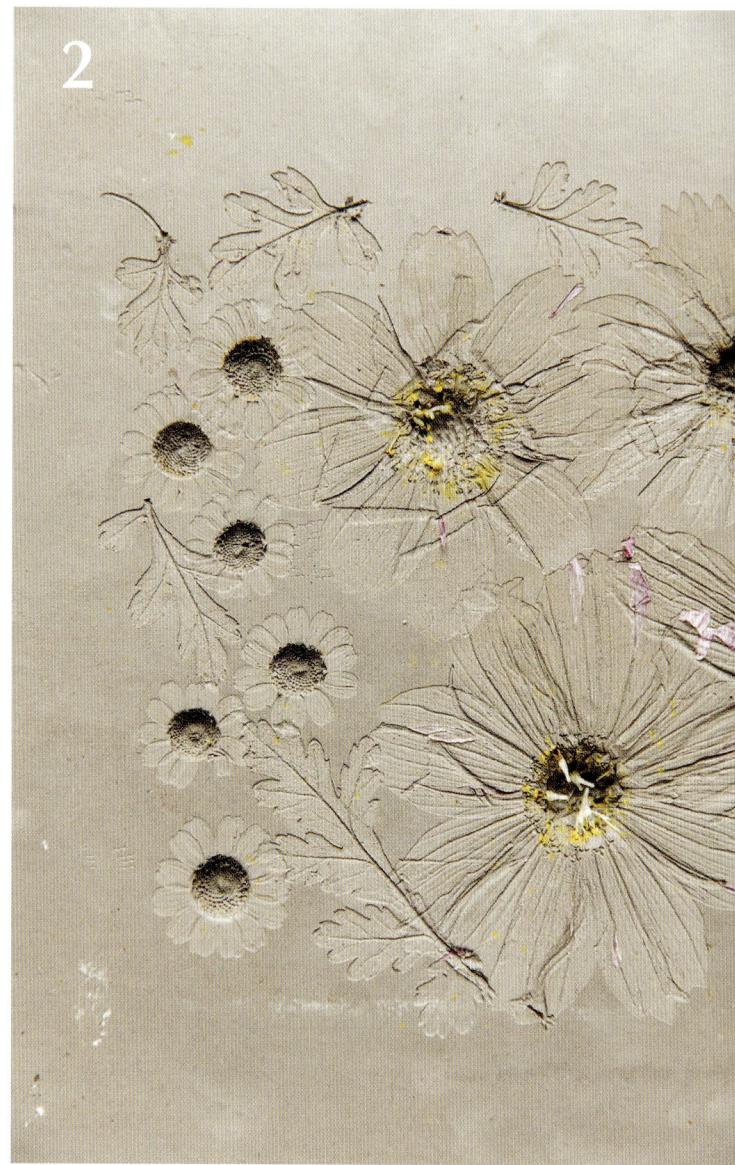

3. After repositioning the frame, seal the edges with clay to ensure that the plaster doesn't leak out.

4. If a small amount of plaster seeps out on to the frame, it's easy to tidy it up with a scalpel blade.

I deliberately left much of the terracotta clay on the surface of the plaster cast and didn't smooth the edges, so that the piece had a rich, textural look.

Nasturtiums

- 15 cm (6 in.) square

- terracotta clay, plaster

- nasturtium (*Tropaeolum* spp.)

One of the first bas-relief castings I painted included nasturtiums, and I attempted to replicate that original here using terracotta clay. For me, nasturtiums always bring to mind a 1920s Japanese aesthetic. I chose to arrange this small collection of flowers and leaves as an abstract pattern, with one flower positioned in profile and the other splayed out to make the flower more recognisable. I pressed both the front and back of the leaves in the clay, as each side has something to offer. The composition entirely fills the square, with some of the elements extending outside the frame, giving the whole composition a certain dynamism.

Nasturtium leaves and flowers lift out of the clay very nicely; however, if rolled and left in the clay for any length of time, they tend to start disintegrating, and then it becomes quite difficult to pull them out. The best idea is to remove them sooner rather than later.

I particularly like using terracotta clay for tiles that I plan to paint. The clay makes a good base colour for painting and helps add more detail and depth to the overall effect.

Instructions

1. Nasturtium flowers and leaves lend themselves well to a more abstract layout.

2. Nasturtium leaves peel off quite easily in one piece.

3. Reposition the frame before sealing the edges with a length of clay.

4. Terracotta clay leaves a lot of colour on the plaster, and you can clean off as much or as little as you like to achieve the final effect.

Wedding bouquet

- 40 cm (15¾ in.) square

- grey clay, plaster

- campanula (*Campanula trachelium*)

- corncockle (*Agrostemma githago* 'Bianca')

- cornflower (*Centaurea cyanus* 'Blue Ball')

- gaura (*Oenothera lindheimeri* 'Summer Breeze')

- goat's rue (*Galega officinalis*)

- phlox (*Phlox drummondii* 'Creme Brulee')

- pincushion flower (*Scabiosa caucasica* 'Goldingensis', *S. atropurpurea* 'Snowmaiden')

- poppy (*Papaver rhoeas* 'Amazing Grey')

- pot marigold (*Calendula officinalis* 'Sherbet Fizz')

- sweet pea (*Lathyrus latifolius* 'White Pearl')

- yarrow (*Achillea millefolium* 'Appleblossom')

This gorgeous selection of flowers was provided by London-based floral designers JamJar Flowers. One of the joys of casting flowers is that you can use them to encapsulate an important moment, and JamJar kindly provided a beautiful summer wedding bouquet collection for me to use in this book. Many wedding bouquets feature roses, but I asked the florist not to include them because roses are really tricky to cast well.

With so many plants provided for the bouquet, I laid them out to see what was included and then began playing around with possibilities. The grey poppy, which is gorgeous, became my keystone plant, and I arranged everything else around it. One of the conundrums when using a large quantity of plants for casting is that it's often tricky to know when to stop. Bear in mind that once the plants are positioned on the clay, it's difficult to remove a plant without making marks on the clay. So take your time, and if in doubt, bear in mind the old adage: "less is more."

If I'm using several of the same plant or similar looking plants, I'll often arrange each of them a slightly different way to offer a composition of the plants' various aspects. For the pincushion flowers, for example, I placed one flower facing upward and another facing downward into the clay. The corncockle made a particularly lovely impression, with the calyx—the part that holds the petals—appearing ridged and striped. The plants formed an undulating design, with the tendrils of the everlasting peas forming the highest point on one side, dipping down to the pot marigold in the centre, and then rising upward to the splayed-out petals of the corncockle.

Most plants pulled out of the clay easily, although the yarrow left behind some debris, which I took the time to remove from the clay.

A botanical bas-relief is perfect for capturing a special memory such as a wedding bouquet.

Instructions

1. A wedding bouquet includes perfect flowers for a botanical bas-relief to make an enduring memento of a special day.

2. When more than one of the same species is included, both sides of the flowers can be used for the impression.

3. After repositioning the frame, you can begin to see how the design works in the space.

4. The plants lifted out of the clay relatively easily, leaving fairly clean impressions.

2

3

4

Other suggestions for summer

These plants can also be used for summer bas-reliefs.

- avens (*Geum* spp.)

- cinquefoil (*Potentilla* spp.)

- columbine (*Aquilegia* spp.)

- delphinium (*Delphinium* spp.)

- fleabane (*Erigeron annuus*)

- iris (*Iris* spp.)

- lavender (*Lavandula* spp.)

- meadow rue (*Thalictrum* spp.)

- mint (*Mentha* spp.)

- nepeta (*Calamintha nepeta*)

- penstemon (*Penstemon* spp.)

Compositions
for Late Summer

As late summer begins, I often panic, thinking that I'm running out of time and I haven't done enough before autumn and winter arrive. That said, it's a beautiful time of year, with a few sunny days still, and the garden has a warm, homey, lived-in look. There's invariably a last blast of rich colour from perennials such as asters, persicarias, sage, and dahlias—the final hurrah—as the leaves start to turn, and you can feel the change of season in the air. The mornings start crisp and chilly, and by the end of the day, the light is golden, helping us ease into winter.

Sage

- **12 cm (4¾ in.) square**
- **grey clay, plaster**
- **sage (*Salvia officinalis*)**

Leonardo da Vinci made a nature print of a sage leaf, which was published in the sixteenth-century *Codex Atlanticus* (*Codice Atlantico*). The impression is beautifully clear and defined, and in terms of inspiration, you can't get better than that! Sage also makes a fine impression in clay and pulls out cleanly, making it an ideal plant to ensure success. I first cast sage many years ago, and I still really like working with it. Casting sage is a great little first project to build up your confidence.

Sage is a very straightforward plant to cast. It's just a matter of finding a nice little sprig to fit the frame and pressing it in. The specimen I used here is a bit chunkier than I usually use, but it's still very nice. I always have in mind "contrast, contrast, contrast", so I used both sides of the leaves, as each side makes a good impression. As usual, I extended the stem past the bottom edge of the frame. Once sage is pressed into the clay, it generally pulls out in one go.

Sage always gives great results
and is easy to work with.

Instructions

1. Lightly place the sage in position, and then replace the frame to check the composition.

2. Some of the leaves are placed face up and others are face down to maximize contrast.

3. Be sure to create a good seal of clay around the outside of the frame before pouring in the plaster.

4. Although the plaster has seeped out over the inside edge of the frame, this is easy to remove in the cleaning process.

The white space above and
between the plants helps draw
attention to their interesting
stems and flowers.

Cyclamens

- 15 cm (6 in.) square

- grey clay, plaster

- cyclamen (*Cyclamen* spp.)

While traveling outside the United Kingdom, I've seen cyclamen growing wild in the spring. They are magical little plants. There's something quite stylised, almost graphic, about them. They are quite upright and geometric in form, and I love their various stages of growth—especially the curve of the stem when it's coiled like a little spring and the delicacy of the bud emerging. Cyclamen flowers appear before the leaves, which can seem quite surreal. I've cast and painted my cyclamen bas-reliefs, and they look lovely with subtle blush colours. In this piece, I used a few leaves and fourteen stems arranged to highlight their various forms—from buds, to flowers, to tightly sprung stems that fling the seeds out into the world.

Instructions

1. It's interesting to see the various stages of cyclamen development—especially the stem, which coils like a little spring after the plant has set seed.

2. Roll the clay nice and flat; you can use a flexible steel scraper to flatten it even more.

3. Cyclamen is small, firm, and maintains its shape well when flattened into the clay.

4. The clay peels off cleanly to reveal the design.

Casting Flowers

A relatively sparse design can
show off a plant's interesting
form to best advantage.

Japanese anemones

- 25 cm (10 in.) square

- grey clay, plaster

- Japanese anemone (*Anemone hupehensis*)

In this fairly minimal arrangement, I used just two stems of anemone. Even then, I thought there were too many offshoots, so I used secateurs to snip some off. Quite a few of the stems had gone to seed and formed little seed-heads, so I removed some of those as well. I didn't want the composition to be overcrowded.

Anemones are easy to cast because the petals are relatively thick and robust and the stems are wiry. The seedhead, however, is puffy in the middle and a bit like cotton wool, so it can easily get stuck in the clay, making it difficult to remove without leaving particles behind. In this project, some of the tiny stamens also got stuck in the clay, but I left them there. There's always an element of chance as to whether or not these details will get picked up in the plaster, and I love that aspect of the process.

When you've put together a minimal layout in terms of plant material, you face more of a risk of a pour mark appearing, as there are fewer places to disguise it. Always try to pour the plaster into the area with the most detail to help hide the pour mark.

Instructions

1. If the stems are too dense, don't be afraid to snip some of them away carefully, ideally close to the base.

2. Take your time when rolling the plants into the clay to ensure that everything is firmly embedded, and use a flexible steel scraper to smooth it out even more.

3. Two separate stems, three flower heads, and five little spherical seedheads are used in this composition.

4. The clay peels off easily and cleanly.

This airy composition benefits
from the clay left behind in
the detail, as it helps delineate
the various elements.

Mixed late-summer arrangement

- 40 cm (15¾ in.) square

- grey clay, plaster

- aster (*Symphyotrichum* spp.)

- black-eyed Susan (*Rudbeckia hirta*)

- cosmos (*Cosmos* spp.)

- dahlia (*Dahlia* spp.)

- dill (*Anethum graveolens*)

- nasturtium (*Tropaeolum* spp.)

- sedum (*Hylotelephium* spp.)

- Siberian melic (*Melica altissima* 'Alba')

- sneezeweed (*Helenium* spp.)

My garden felt very "end-of-season" at the time I created this arrangement, but I used what I had, including a dark dahlia, the ornamental grass *Melica altissima* 'Alba', and other late-season plants. As is often the case at this time of year, lots of flowers in purples and yellows were blooming in my garden.

I positioned the plants in an intuitive, free-form way. The dahlias were a challenge. Their flowerheads are quite full, and the petals tended to splay out and disengage when I rolled them flat. To avoid this as best I could, I pinned them down with my fingers as I passed the rolling pin over the top so that they didn't escape. The seedheads of the Siberian melic, which are like miniature grains of rice, tended to get stuck in the clay but were easy to remove. The petals of the aster are quite delicate, tricky to extract, and they make only a faint impression.

Instructions

1. Fine petals, parts of the stamen, and seedheads are the trickiest bits to remove from the clay.

2. Though it's a good idea to remove as much of the plant material as possible, you can leave in some bits to add to the charm of the final piece.

3. Once the plaster is thoroughly set and you've peeled off the clay, you can take off the frame immediately or do it later.

Other suggestions for late summer

These late-summer plants are good options for botanical bas-reliefs.

- amaranth (*Amaranthus* spp.)

- crimson flag lily (*Hesperantha coccinea*)

- cup and saucer vine (*Cobaea scandens*)

- false bishop's weed (*Ammi majus*)

- montbretia (*Crocosmia* spp.)

- persicaria (*Persicaria* spp.)

- red-hot poker (*Kniphofia* spp.)

- white laceflower (*Orlaya grandiflora*)

Compositions for Autumn

For many of us, autumn is all about leaves and the variations in their shapes, colours, and textures. It is the perfect time of year to appreciate the beauty of acorns, catkins, and seedheads such as the winged fruits of sycamores. Along with these I also like using what's left of hedgerow brambles, including the leaves and the little hard, red fruit—because they are unripe, they contain little, if any, juice and so are fairly easy to cast. For me, spending time seeking out and gathering plants in the garden and in the wild is a hugely enjoyable and important part of the process.

A small study of autumn
leaves.

Mixed autumn leaves

- 12 cm (4¾ in.) square

- terracotta clay, plaster

- common beech (*Fagus sylvatica*) leaves

- hawthorn (*Crataegus monogyna*) leaves

- maple (*Acer* spp.) leaves

- oak (*Quercus* spp.) leaves

This cast is basically an intimate study of a selection of small autumn leaves and the contrast of their various forms and textures. The process of choosing and positioning the leaves is really important to me, and although the varying colours won't translate into the clay, I did have in mind that I might paint this one, which informed the layout. I have previously painted casts of leaves and the end results can look very pretty. I chose to use terracotta clay because the colour is beautifully rich, like the shades of autumn.

I placed the leaves as if I'd found them scattered on the ground. I did consider how best to overlap them, so some leaves were placed under others. Unlike many of the designs I create, for this piece, the stems of the leaves didn't necessarily fall over the edges of the frame. The leaves were relatively easy to pull out of the clay, making this a great project for beginners.

For me, studies such as this work well on a small scale. They don't always translate as well to a bigger piece, unless you're going for a wallpaper effect.

1

2

Instructions

1. These small autumn leaves are placed in an abstract pattern, almost as they'd be found on the ground.

2. When the leaves are rolled flat into the clay, the outline of the frame can disappear slightly, but you should be able to see enough of the frame outline to use as a guide for repositioning it.

3. The leaves pull out really easily, though placing stems over the inner edge of the outline of the frame always helps.

With smaller designs, I generally prefer to fill as much of the space as possible with plants.

Maple sprig

- **15 cm (6 in.) square**
- **terracotta clay, plaster**
- **maple (*Acer* spp.)**

This small stem of maple leaves nicely filled out the small area of the bas-relief. I placed the sprig on the clay to look as though it had fallen naturally. I simply pressed the leaves into place and made sure that the slightly bent stem extended beyond the edge of the frame outline.

Maple leaves can produce a faint and delicate impression, so much of the artistry of this casting lies in the cleanup process. It's important to leave just enough of the clay to bring out the detail of the leaf edges and veins. I particularly liked the twig, which had an interesting texture and added subtle detail. The whole thing sits fairly snugly within the frame, with an even amount of space around the perimeter.

After they were pressed into the clay, the stems and leaves lifted out easily, so there was a minimal amount of cleaning up to do.

Instructions

1. A single stem of delicate maple leaves fills the entire area.

2. Roll the fine leaves and stems into the clay.

3. The veining on the undersides of the leaves makes a fine but distinct impression.

4. I like the contrast between the deep mark made by the stem and the more subtle marks left by the leaves.

For me, this piece with the
acorns, blackberries, and
sycamore perfectly sums up
autumn.

Brambles and leaves

- 25 cm (10 in.) square

- terracotta clay, plaster

- blackberry (*Rubus* spp.) bramble

- fern leaf

- oak (*Quercus* spp.) leaf and acorn

- sycamore maple (*Acer pseudoplatanus*) leaf and winged seeds

Quite often, a design for a botanical bas-relief will begin when I choose a specimen that I really love. In this case, a fern in my garden first caught my attention. In nearby hedgerows, I came across a curved bramble branch, complete with hard, unripened blackberries, and I thought the two would work well together. In fact, the little stem of bramble was of particular interest because the undersides of the leaves were dotted with little black spots, and I wanted to capture these in the clay. I also included a single maple leaf and its winged seeds, as well as a small oak leaf and acorn. Overall, I thought it worked out well in a pleasingly pared back, minimal sort of a way.

I positioned the fern and the bramble stem so that they slightly curved inward from either side, with the leaves of the bramble taking up the central space. I then positioned the maple leaf and seeds at the base of the bramble and the oak leaf centrally, toward the bottom of the frame. When using acorns, I like to smear them with a little petroleum jelly before placing them to make it a little easier to remove them from the clay.

After using a rolling pin to flatten the foliage and berries into the clay, I pushed the acorn into the clay in such a way that it was only half submerged, rather than being flush with the surface—think of it as an impression of half of the acorn. The same technique would work if you were using pine cones or large rose hips, for example. In this instance, all the material popped out of the clay relatively easily.

Instructions

1. The combination of stems, leaves, berries, and an acorn forms an interesting mix of contrasting forms and textures.

2. Replacing the frame before removing the plant matter helps you check that the design works as well as possible and whether any additional material is needed.

3. This piece celebrates the beauty of imperfection by including the black spots on the bramble leaves that were picked up in the clay.

4. The hard, unripe fruit of the bramble leaves a distinctive impression.

Casting Flowers

This large autumn display
includes a mix of leaves,
berries, seeds, and catkins that
I found growing wild in my
neighbourhood.

Rose hips, beech, and bramble

- 40 cm (15¾ in.) square

- grey clay, plaster

- blackberry (*Rubus* spp.) bramble

- common beech (*Fagus sylvatica*) leaves

- dandelion (*Taraxacum officinale*) flower and seedhead

- hazel (*Corylus avellana*) catkins

- rose (*Rosa* spp.) hip and leaves

- stinging nettle (*Urtica dioica*) leaves

- sycamore maple (*Acer pseudoplatanus*) leaves

- yew (*Taxus baccata*)

In this arrangement, I particularly love how the yellow beech leaves combine with the bramble, the maple leaves, and the yew to provide an interesting mix of shapes and forms. I also included a dandelion flower and seedhead as they have a unique charm too. The dandelion stem is rounded and quite crunchy and doesn't keep its form when rolled flat into the clay. Because dandelions have a tendency to splay out and leave wet sap on the clay, be mindful to keep the roller and clay clean while working with them.

The stinging nettle leaves are quite papery but are highly textured and make a nice impression. However, they are also quite fine and should be pulled out of the clay shortly after they've been rolled in. If they're left in the clay for too long, they quickly start to disintegrate and are tricky to remove. Be sure to wear gloves to protect your skin while picking and handling them. As the rose hip was rather small, I simply rolled it in with the other plants; if it were larger, I would have done it on a second pass, only half pressed into the clay. Yew is an ancient plant with lots of interesting uses medicinally and makes a lovely impression, but I don't use it often—maybe because it's relatively stiff and I'm more drawn to soft, wispy things that have a bit more potential to curve into the design. Catkins also make a lovely addition to a display; however, to cast them in bas-relief, you should avoid those that are loosely formed and crumbly. I was lucky and found some that were nice and firm and therefore didn't leave much debris behind in the clay. Everything else pulled out fairly easily too.

Instructions

1. When including catkins in a bas-relief, choose those that are relatively firm; if they are too crumbly, they will disintegrate when flattened.

2. Dandelions are quite crunchy and exude a lot of sap when rolled into the clay.

3. Use a scalpel blade to remove any remaining material, such as this rose hip, which is firmly lodged in the clay.

4. Even with bigger pieces, the clay peels off easily, and although quite a lot of plaster may leak out onto the frame, it's easy to remove during the cleaning process.

Casting Flowers

Other suggestions for autumn

These plants can also be used for autumn bas-reliefs.

- borage (*Borago officinalis*)
- cape lily (*Nerine* spp.)
- common ivy (*Hedera helix*) leaves
- golden clematis (*Clematis tangutica*)
- hawthorn (*Crataegus monogyna*) leaves and berries
- heuchera (*Heuchera* spp.)
- holly (*Ilex* spp.) leaves and berries
- Russian sage (*Salvia yangii*)
- Virginia creeper (*Parthenocissus quinquefolia*)
- wild roses (*Rosa* spp.)

Compositions for Winter

With the seasons varying so much from year to year, winter is something of a moveable feast, and I find it tricky to define precisely what "winter plants" are. When I started out casting plants, I assumed I wouldn't find anything of much value to cast in the winter, and it was wonderful to discover that a surprising number of plants look really beautiful at this time of year. When plants dry out and foliage dies back, often their sculptural qualities are revealed, and these can lend themselves well to casting. I also find that among all the old and dead plants, any signs of new life emerging are eye-catching. There is often something very pure, almost poetic, about plants that bloom in winter.

Snowdrops make a particularly good project for beginners because they reliably produce good results.

Snowdrops

- 12 cm (4¾ in.) square

- grey clay, plaster

- snowdrops (*Galanthus* spp.)

Snowdrops are lovely little things that cast exceptionally well. The petals have a waxy nature, and they hold much of their form even when pressed down into the clay. The fact that they are already white also helps you work out how the casting will turn out—as opposed to, say, pansies, whose intrinsic beauty comes from their wonderfully rich colours.

This small bas-relief tile has quite a straightforward design with a small grouping of sweet little snowdrops in a naturalistic pose. I made sure to position their leaves so that they pointed upward at a slight angle and their nodding heads face down in different directions, just as you would find them in the garden. There's something rather lovely about multiples of the same plant, and although I used three snowdrops for this small tile, you could use many more snowdrops on a much bigger scale, such as in a long, narrow tile.

When picking snowdrops, be mindful that the slim, straplike leaves separate from the stem of the flower, so it's best to check how many leaves each bulb produces in the garden and replicate that in your composition. I once made a casting of snowdrops and everyone kept asking me if they were insects or bees, so I suspect the way I positioned them looked atypical. My rule of thumb is always to let the plants guide me rather than forcing them into a particular pose; that way, they invariably look comfortable.

When pressing in the flowers, I separate some of the outer petals (segments) to partly reveal the interior petals. The flowers and leaves are fairly robust, but take care that you don't damage them while pressing them into the clay. The stems are quite strong and wiry, so they lift out relatively easily in one go.

When cleaning up the finished piece, I decided to leave a bit of the grey clay behind in the details rather than wipe and scrub everything super clean. The clay's colour lends itself well to the understated beauty of the snowdrops, and I like the way it subtly outlines and emphasises their shapes and forms.

Instructions

1. When positioning snowdrops, place flowers so that they face different directions, and include the same number of leaves with the stems that you find in nature.

2. Push the flowerheads very gently into the clay to help pin them into position and stop them from moving when rolled into the clay.

3. Start in the centre of the piece and roll up and down, as well as from side to side, so that the material is nicely embedded in the clay.

4. The stems and flower heads lift out cleanly.

5. After repositioning the frame, seal the edges with lengths of clay before pouring the plaster into the area with the most detail.

6. The clay is particularly easy to peel off smaller pieces.

Although it may seem like there's not much to cast during winter, winter weeds make a lovely subject.

Winter weeds

- 12 cm (4¾ in.) square
- grey clay, plaster
- bristly oxtongue (*Helminthotheca echioides*)
- buckthorn plantain (*Plantago lanceolata*)
- sticky willy/cleavers (*Galium aparine*)

Nick Fraser, head gardener at Nunnington Hall in Yorkshire, once told me that if you don't like a weed in your garden, just think of it as a wildflower instead. I love that. It took me a while to discover the charm of winter weeds. Once I'd taken a closer look, I realised that they have some very interesting forms and textures, and I have become particularly fond of using in my compositions plants that are all too often overlooked. Although not featured in this arrangement, stinging nettle (*Urtica dioica*) is among my favourite plants; its serrated leaves and strong stems cast exceptionally well. I'd recommend giving it a go, and (again) be sure to wear gloves while handling them.

In this bas-relief, I broke my usual rule of using just a single specimen on a small tile and managed to pack in a surprising number of different plants. These weeds were growing around my neighbourhood, including bristly oxtongue, which has interesting long, narrow, oblong leaves with lots of lovely lumps and bumps on the surface—a bit like the skin of a toad. There were no flowers to use, but because the plants had plenty of different textures, the composition is interesting nevertheless. Bear in mind that, as a general rule, the more textured the plant's surface, the better it will cast.

When arranging the various leaves, I focused on those with particularly good undersides, which is often where the details of the veins are most prominent. Then I positioned the rest of the plants, weaving them into layers until I was happy with the composition.

All of these plants lifted out of the clay quite cleanly. Sometimes the thicker stems can leave behind a bit of a ragged edge of excess clay. You can simply cut away the excess clay with a scalpel.

Instructions

1. When arranging a selection of leaves, check which sides are the most interesting and place them in the clay first.

2. Including different shapes and textures helps ensure that the composition is dynamic and interesting.

3. Pour the plaster onto the area with the most detail to help hide the pour mark.

4. After removing the clay, it's a good idea to let the plaster dry out thoroughly before working on it.

Although I cleaned off much of the terracotta clay, I left quite a lot to emphasize the detailed parts of the hydrangea.

Hydrangea seedhead

- 12 cm (4¾ in.) square
- terracotta clay, plaster
- hydrangea (*Hydrangea* spp.)

I am drawn to using living material in my work, but dead plants can also make interesting subjects. Winter provides a treasure trove of seedheads, grasses, branches, twigs, and stems. Be mindful not to choose things that will leave an excessive amount of debris behind when you pull them out of the clay, as it can be difficult to remove and you can inadvertently damage a lot of the detail in the process.

In this composition, I used a single stem of a dried hydrangea with a flower-head. I particularly liked its skeletal form. I made the impression in terracotta clay, as its warm reddish colour lends itself particularly well to winter subjects and is almost the same colour as the hydrangea.

I set the stem of the hydrangea at a slight angle, falling over the edge of the square; it's very rare that I place a plant in a bolt-upright position. Fortunately, the stem had retained a number of the flower petals, and I pressed these face down into the clay. The hydrangea fills the tile and, unusually, I didn't leave much space above it. Because of the hydrangea's airy quality, I felt more space wasn't needed.

As with most dried plants, the hydrangea stem is relatively brittle, and parts of it remained embedded in the clay after the main part was lifted out. Whether you use a scalpel or tweezers, it's important that you take your time to lift out the plant matter as carefully as possible and try not to touch the clay with your fingers. I find it helpful to replace the frame and use it as a support to help lever my hand above the clay. You don't have to be fanatical about removing everything, and if little bits are left in the clay, they can often make interesting and unique additions to the final piece.

Instructions

1. When using a single sprig, place it in the clay at a slight angle rather than bolt upright.

2. Dried plants generally leave quite a lot of debris behind in the clay; take your time to pick out what you can.

3. Once the edges of the frame are nicely sealed with clay, you can pour in the plaster.

4. With the terracotta clay removed from the plaster, you can begin to consider how much or how little of the clay you want to clean off the bas-relief.

For this design, I wanted
the background to be clean
and smooth to offset the fine
detail of these winter blooms
outlined in grey clay.

Mixed winter flowers

- 40 cm (15¾ in.) square

- grey clay, plaster

- daffodil (*Narcissus* spp.)

- hellebore (*Helleborus* spp.)

- holly (*Ilex* spp.) seedhead

- magnolia (*Magnolia* spp.) branch and buds

- mahonia (*Mahonia* spp.)

- primrose (*Primula* spp.)

- snowdrop (*Galanthus* spp.)

- snowflake (*Leucojum* spp.)

- viburnum (*Viburnum* × *bodnantense*)

It may sound obvious, but when you opt for a bigger frame and use more plants, you'll have more decisions to make about where to position everything. Here, I used a stem of hellebore flowers as my main feature and placed it first. Hellebore is pretty robust and makes a good impression in the clay. I positioned the flowers facing downward, as I find the interior details more interesting than the back sides. Next, I positioned the snowflake and the primrose, and then continued to build up the composition with the remaining plants, placing them into the clay and weaving the various elements above and below until I created a pleasing composition.

You can see how the snowdrop petals overlap the hellebore and the stem of the viburnum is on top of one of the primrose leaves. The idea is to get a mix of details from the plants in the back as well as those in the front, showing each plant to its best advantage. I left some space at the top of the piece to allow the composition to breathe. Without that space, the layout would have felt overly congested.

Some of the stamens and fine petals remained in the clay after I'd removed the plants, but they were relatively easy to remove with a scalpel blade. One of the issues to be aware of when you're using plants with long, thick stems (such as those of hellebore) is that they can leave a ragged impression when you pull them from the clay. Generally, I try to tidy up the edges as much as I can by using a scalpel blade on an angle to remove the excess clay and gently smooth the edges of the impression.

Instructions

1. Build up the composition gradually, because once a plant is placed on the clay it may leave a mark if you try to remove it.

2. With larger pieces, a long rolling pin is helpful, but you can also manage with a smaller one.

3. The area with the most detail is often near the base of the work, where the stems are most dense, and this is a good place to pour in the plaster.

4. When the clay is peeled off, invariably much of it will remain on the surface and in the details of the plaster; it's up to you to decide how much clay to remove.

Other suggestions for winter

These plants also make wonder winter bas-reliefs.

- Algerian iris (*Iris unguicularis*)

- old man's beard (*Clematis vitalba*)

- sweet box (*Sarcococca* spp.)

- winter aconite (*Eranthis hyemalis*)

- winter-flowering clematis (*C. cirrhosa*)

- witch-hazel (*Hamamelis* spp.)

Botanical Bas-Relief
Out in the World

I have been commissioned to create botanical bas-reliefs for private homes, restaurants, fashion boutiques, and exhibition spaces. When I started out, I worked on a small scale—tiles of 12 cm (4¾ in.) square—but now I enjoy working on a far greater scale to create large landscapes. My biggest panels measured 200 cm (78¾ in.). I love collaborating with designers, being inspired by their vision, and working to their design briefs, and it's fascinating seeing my work applied to different spaces in all sorts of ways, from the ceiling to the floor. I find that bringing nature inside invariably softens a space, and being able to see the simple detail of flowers and foliage without the distraction of colour adds to a sense of calmness.

I also enjoy incorporating meaning into my work. I often do this in a subtle way, so that no one but the client knows the particular significance of the plants I've used. Sometimes I'm asked to incorporate sentimental or significant items into a composition. I see this type of commission as a form of family portrait. I'm helping record memories for my clients.

The dining area at HIDE displays twelve panels that create an uneven crenelation.

HIDE restaurant, Piccadilly, London

I was approached by interior designer Rose Murray of These White Walls, who was looking for original work for a bespoke restaurant in the heart of central London. Rose was interested in commissioning large panels that would combine a botanical theme with objects significant to those working at the restaurant. Whilst I'd previously cast both plants and objects, this was the first time I'd united both together in a single piece. The design brief outlined that I was to incorporate the objects in a subtle way, so they weren't immediately obvious within the composition of the plants. I was given all sorts of things to include in the casting—jewellery, building blocks, sweets, and even a little statue of a Buddha. Apart from a necklace belonging to the head chef, Ollie Dabbous, I wasn't told to whom all the other objects belonged.

Creatively, I was given free rein, although I had to work to the dimensions of the panels. I ended up placing Ollie's necklace in the area where I cast all the edible plants. Interestingly, these plants were sourced from the gardens at Raymond Blanc's restaurant, Le Manoir aux Quat'Saisons, in Oxfordshire. I decided to check to be sure that there was no conflict of interest in using plants from one restaurant for a commission by another. To my relief, Ollie happened to be a protégé of the legendary Chef Blanc. I think we all really enjoyed that unexpected synchronicity!

For one area of the restaurant, I created twelve panels that linked together to form a kind of uneven crenelation, like the top of a castle. They featured a wide range of plants that I'd picked between early summer and late autumn. For the second area, the designer wanted to reference the fact that the restaurant over-looks Green Park, so I created a section of four panels featuring London plane trees, to echo those visible from the windows.

I completed the work in November, and HIDE opened in April of the following year. It was fun being so playful, and I enjoy looking back at the project and thinking about what plants came from where and the little stories associated with all the various elements. I hope the panels capture memories and mementoes of a particular time for all those who work there.

Hidcote Manor garden, Gloucestershire

Sarah Malleson, who at the time was head gardener at Hidcote, the National Trust's iconic garden in Gloucestershire, had spotted a feature about my work in *Gardens Illustrated* magazine and loved it. Some years later, Sarah was working in the visitor experience team, and she invited me to cast plants from the garden over the course of a year, culminating in a solo exhibition.

The design brief was perfect: I could choose the plants and cast them at whatever size I wanted! I could rummage through the flowerbeds and take what I liked. In all, I created twenty-two pieces, all cast in plaster, with the smallest being 12 cm (4¾ in.) square and the largest at 100 cm × 65 cm (39⅓ in. × 25½ in.). I made moulds of several pieces so I could reproduce the design in various colours. I also made some concrete pieces that were sold in the shop. It was important for me that visitors to the exhibition were able to identify the plants in the castings, so I also made some illustrations with a corresponding list of plant names to go alongside them.

One of the twenty-two bas-reliefs I made of plants growing at Hidcote, the iconic English garden in Gloucestershire.

Mayfair apartments, London

The owner of a private apartment block in Mayfair had been inspired by the pieces I'd made for HIDE, which is just around the corner. These panels were made from a mould and were embedded into the walls. There were fifteen wall panels in total, and it was the first time that I'd made a ceiling rose and twelve corner ceiling panels. I found the project really exciting, because I was creating my personal take on something that is usually quite traditional—though my work was definitely not a pastiche, as I wasn't trying to make my pieces look like eighteenth-century plaster cornicing. I worked with the architectural firm HUT on the design, and the installation was skilfully managed by the construction company Volute.

Each panel measured 130 cm × 65 cm (51 in. × 25½ in.), and I had five different designs to combine in a variety of ways. Although the panels are not unique casts, I made them as a limited edition. The plants represented the height of summer and included cosmos (*Cosmos* spp.), fennel (*Foeniculum* spp.), gaura (*Oenothera* spp.), heuchera (*Heuchera* spp.), meadow rue (*Thalictrum* spp.), passion flower (*Passiflora* spp.), red-hot poker (*Kniphofia* spp.), sedum (*Sedum* spp.), and sweet pea (*Lathyrus* spp.). I'd grown most of these plants, but I also included others that were given to me by my good friend Patricia.

The panels, which are basically a contemporary version of traditional cornicing and plaster stucco decoration, are embedded seamlessly in the wall so that just the relief shows.

Arit Anderson garden, RHS Chelsea Flower Show

Garden designer and television presenter Arit Anderson came across my work at Royal Horticultural Society Hampton Court Palace in the summer of 2021. She'd seen some bricks I'd made to decorate part of the path element for Dutch designer Carien van Boxtel's cut flower garden. Arit was in the process of creating "Garden of Hope", a show garden at RHS Chelsea Flower Show a few months later. She was really keen to record the plants she'd used, and she liked the idea of commissioning a triptych, with one panel in full colour.

Unusually that year, because of COVID restrictions, the show had been moved from its traditional week in May to September, so I was working with autumnal plants such as salvia, meadow rue, and dahlias. Because of their soft petals, casting dahlias is never easy!

It was a privilege to work with Arit, who completely understood that my role was not unlike a court painter (an artist who painted for members of a royal family). I was charged with keeping an accurate record of an event that had been so important and significant for her.

Jardin Blanc, RHS Chelsea Flower Show

The renowned chef Raymond Blanc created Jardin Blanc, a special pop-up restaurant at the RHS Chelsea Flower Show. It was a hidden wonder, sectioned off from the public area of the event. Each year at the show, the restaurant had showcased artists. In 2017, their design team approached me to create a piece.

I remember going to Le Manoir aux Quat'Saisons (Blanc's world-renowned restaurant in Oxfordshire) when I was sixteen years old as a special treat with my parents. I still have a photo of me among the colourful rows of chard, which I loved. I asked if I could go to the Oxfordshire kitchen garden to select edible plants to cast. The head gardener was very helpful, and having access to such great plants was like a dream come true. I used a wide range of edibles, including beetroot, amaranth, fennel, cabbage, sorrel, and lettuce, plus edible flowers such as marigold and borage. This was the first time I'd created a specific collection of themed pieces. I later learned that Queen Elizabeth II attended high tea where my work was hanging, so I'd like to think that she also enjoyed them!

One of three botanical bas-relief panels that formed the triptych I created for Arit Anderson.

This panel using the plants from Le Manoir aux Quat'Saisons was made in the style of Wedgwood, with white detail against a blue background, and included fennel, chicory, amaranth, marigold, and nasturtium.

Restaurant Andrew Fairlie, Gleneagles, Scotland

The interior designer who was working on refurbishing this restaurant contacted me about creating some pieces for the restaurant, and I subsequently spoke with the owner, Kate Fairlie, who is Andrew's widow. I was asked to make three horizontal panels for a spot above the fireplace, and, unusually, the plants should appear to grow downward, as opposed to upward, which is how I usually position flowers in my work. Initially, we discussed using ivy because the restaurant is dark and plush, but we later decided it would look a bit too gothic. Eventually, we settled on grapevines.

I was sent plants mainly taken from the restaurant's garden, including a wonderful strawberry vine as well as other edibles and herbs such as bay leaves, nasturtiums, turnip, fennel, lemon verbena, sage, and micro vegetables such as tiny leeks. The vines featured in the upper panels hang downward, while the edibles and herbs are placed in the bottom panel. It was a challenge to make sure that the plants were aligned from one panel to the next.

Opposite: The pale plaster bas-relief brings a calm luminosity to the dark restaurant.

Following: The two panels were mounted side by side in a single frame.

The Dorchester Hotel, Hyde Park, London

This famous five-star luxury hotel in London, opened in 1931, was undergoing a major refurbishment. I'd been contacted through a design company that was commissioning new artworks for the hotel. For the downstairs promenade, I was asked to make two panels, each 65 cm × 145 cm (25½ in. × 57 in.), which they wanted to be painted in watercolours. The colour palette was restricted to hues of green, yellow, orange, and subtle blue. The deadline was relatively early in the year, and I had a limited selection of plants growing in my garden. However, after a successful trip to London's legendary New Covent Garden Flower Market, I returned with delphiniums, buttercups, daisies, and fritillaries, which looked pretty together.

Private residence, London

I was contacted via my Instagram account by a woman who asked me to create two bespoke casts for her home. Her children had grown up in the house in London's Islington district, but she knew that the family might be moving at some point. As a future memento, she asked me to make casts of branches of the fig and mulberry trees from her garden. She suggested the proportions of the final pieces, although as is invariably the case, the size was largely dictated by her chosen plants.

Neither the fig nor the mulberry were in full fruit when I cast them, which worked to my advantage, because it would have been very difficult to cast squishy, ripe fruits. I found that the fig leaves' detail held exceptionally well and made a lovely impression. As yet, she has not moved from her home, so the fig and the mulberry castings are currently still hanging as a diptych there.

The two commissioned pieces, leaves from a fig and a mulberry, work well together and are hung side by side in the client's house.

Private residence, Wisconsin

I was commissioned by Jessica Jubelirer Design to create ceiling panels of botanical bas-reliefs for a private residence in Wisconsin. The designer approached me with a pattern in mind. I thought that it would be fantastic if all the plants looked as if they were growing in from the edges of the panels, with the centres of each panel being blank. The ceiling consisted of three separate areas, and I made eighteen panels in total. This wonderful interior design was featured in *Architectural Digest*.

The ceiling panels for this private residence run the length of the corridor.

Hannah's birthday present

My niece, Hannah, gave me a bunch of flowers from her grandmother's garden. For her eighteenth birthday, she wanted a permanent reminder of the summers she had spent there. These summer plants were typical of those growing in a cottage garden and included bleeding-hearts (*Dicentra* spp.), clematis (*Clematis* spp.), lavender (*Lavandula* spp.), montbretia (*Crocosmia* spp.), mullein (*Verbascum* spp.), poppy (*Papaver* spp.), and sage (*Salvia* spp.).

I enjoy creating special pieces that hold so much meaning at a particular moment in time.

Casting Flowers

Recommended Reading

A number of technical books focus on plaster casting, but none deal specifically with casting with plants—neither practical guides nor the history of this art form. The closest art form is nature printing, a technique in which the surface of a natural object is used to produce a print. These are my reading recommendations for both plaster casting and nature printing.

Bethmann, Laura Donnelly. 2011. *Hand Printing from Nature: Create Unique Prints from Fabric, Paper, and Other Surfaces Using Natural and Found Materials.* North Adams, MA: Storey Publishing.

Bethmann, Laura Donnelly. 1996. *Nature Printing with Herbs, Fruits & Flowers.* North Adams, MA: Storey Publishing.

Brooks, Nick. 2005. *Mouldmaking and Casting: A Technical Manual.* Ramsbury, Wiltshire, U.K.: The Crowood Press Ltd.

Brooks, Nick. 2011. *Advanced Mould Making and Casting.* Ramsbury, Wiltshire, U.K.: The Crowood Press Ltd.

Cave, Roderick. 2010. *Impressions of Nature: A History of Nature Printing.* London: British Library Division.

Guralnick, Margot. 2012. The Ultimate Pressed Flowers. *Gardenista,* gardenista.com/posts/the-ultimate-pressed-flowers.

Harvey, Stephanie. 2016. *Creative Plasterwork: 25 Beautiful Projects Shown Step by Step.* London: Lorenz Books.

Martin, Andrew. 2007. *The Essential Guide to Mold Making & Slip Casting.* New York: Union Square & Co.

Nature Printing Society and S. Huffman. 2016. *The Art of Printing from Nature: 40th Anniversary Edition.* Minneapolis: Nature Printing Society. Kindle.

Richardson, Melissa, and Amy Fielding. 2022. *The Modern Flower Press: Capturing the Beauty of Nature.* New York: Henry N. Abrams.

Tocha, Veronika. 2019. *Near Life: The Gipsformerie: 200 Years of Casting in Plaster.* Munich: Prestel.

Townsend, Jen, and Renée Zettle-Stirling. 2017. *Cast: Art and Objects Made Using Humanity's Most Transformational Process.* Atglen, PA: Schiffer Publishing Ltd.

Zucker, Matthew, and Pia Öslund. 2023. *Capturing Nature: 150 Years of Nature Printing.* Hudson, NY: Princeton Architectural Press.

Acknowledgments

When I pressed my first plant into clay to begin the process of what I call botanical bas-relief, I had no idea how my artwork would evolve and what impact it would have on my life. Over the years, I've been grateful to so many people who have been incredibly supportive and helped me in a variety of ways. I'll begin within my local community and fellow mums at the primary school (a long time ago now!). My number one gardening buddy, Patricia Major, and designer Leslie Mello. It was Leslie who introduced me to Michelle McKenna, who gave me my first commission, for which I'll always be grateful. A huge thank you to *Gardenista* gardening blog, whose write-up helped to introduce my work across the online world, and to *Gardens Illustrated* magazine. To this day, I meet people who mention Sorrel Everton's lovely article called "First Impressions".

That piece for *Gardens Illustrated* was commissioned by Juliet Roberts, who now, over ten years on, is the writer of this book. Working from her home in France, Juliet has been so incredibly patient and focused as she has listened to me talking about my work and how I do what I do. She has managed to whittle down hours of online conversations into a wonderful description and presentation of my practice. I have been so lucky to have photographer Éva Németh record me and my work over the course of the four seasons. She has brilliantly captured my working process and all the pieces in various stages of completion.

This book would never have happened without meeting Stacee Lawrence at London's RHS Chelsea Flower Show. Stacee, who was then working with Timber Press, was so enthusiastic about the potential of a collaboration. So was I, and it's been a real pleasure working with the current team at Hachette Book Group, including editor Makenna Goodman and photo editor Sarah Milhollin.

My stand at the RHS Chelsea Flower Show has been a magnet for meeting so many wonderful people in the botanical world, and I want to send out a big thank you to all the friends who have helped me during the week of the flower show. It was at Chelsea that I first met the Dutch garden designer Carien van Boxtel. Her friendship and support have been amazing, and I was thrilled to have contributed my work to her show gardens at RHS Hampton Court Palace. Through Carien I was introduced to Arit Anderson, garden designer and wonderful presenter on the BBC TV programme *Gardeners' World*, and I even got to cast some of the flowers in a gorgeous garden she created for the Chelsea Flower Show.

I am also incredibly grateful to artists Allegra Fitzherbert and Kitty Rice. I met Kitty through the superb JamJar Flowers, which has commissioned pieces from me over the years. Kitty then introduced me to Allegra. I am very fortunate to have had such talented artists working for me as assistants.

Finally, what can I say but a huge thank you to my children, who have grown up in a house crammed with bags of plaster and casts of all sizes almost everywhere! It may not be a typical home, but it's been our lives for many years! A special thank you to my sisters, Sara and Julia, and my mother, Marina, who gave me my love of plants, and my late father, Barry, who instilled in me a love of art. And last but not least, to my husband, Alan, who is convinced that he is my number one fan!

Index

About the Authors

EVA NÉMETH

Rachel Dein studied fine art at Middlesex University and then trained as a prop maker for the English National Opera. She also worked as a freelancer for fifteen years at numerous theatres and museums, including Madame Tussauds, the Royal Opera House, and Shakespeare's Globe in London. Throughout this time, she continued to work on personal art projects. Having stopped freelancing to look after her three young children, she began casting small plaster tiles in her home studio. She exhibited her work at a local gallery and immediately began getting commissions for her botanical bas-reliefs. Her art has been published in *ELLE Decoration*, *House & Garden*, *Vogue*, *Architectural Digest*, *Gardens Illustrated*, *Period Living*, *Country Life*, *The Daily Telegraph*, *Martha Stewart Living*, *The Irish Times*, and *Gardenista*. Recent books that feature her work include *In Bloom: Creatwing and Living with Flowers* by Ngoc Minh Ngo; *Cast: Art and Objects Made Using Humanity's Most Transformational Process* by Jen Townsend and Renée Zettle-Sterling; and *The Botanical Bible: Plants, Flowers, Art, Recipes & Other Home Uses* by Sonya Patel Ellis. Her work has been exhibited at Cambridge Darkroom Gallery, Ben Uri Gallery, Hampstead School of Art, and the Aga Khan Centre Gallery. Rachel has exhibited at the RHS Chelsea Flower Show in London for almost a decade. She was artist-in-residence for the National Trust's Hidcote Manor Gardens in 2018–2019 and for Nunnington Hall in 2022–2023. Her website is RachelDein.com.

Juliet Roberts is a freelance garden journalist, creative director, and lecturer based in the southwest of France. She is passionate about plants, art, and contemporary crafts and is keen to encourage more people to garden, spend time outdoors discovering the wonders of nature, and use creativity as a form of mindfulness. As editor of *Gardens Illustrated* magazine for more than thirteen years, she has not only seen more remarkable gardens than most, but she's also developed a wide knowledge of garden-related art. In 2012, she discovered and fell in love with Rachel Dein's work and immediately contacted her to arrange a feature in the magazine. Since then, Juliet has eagerly followed Rachel's progress and always makes a point of visiting Rachel's stand at the world-renowned RHS Chelsea Flower Show, where Juliet is regularly a show garden judge.

About the Photographer

Éva Németh is an internationally published photographer specialising in all things gardens. This passion started whilst spending most of her childhood in her grandmother's garden. Later, this love for gardens and flowers was combined with another passion of hers: photography. She works with some of the United Kingdom's best garden designers and floral artists, and her work is regularly featured in magazines such as *House & Garden* and *Gardens Illustrated*. She has worked on other books all centred around gardens, flowers, and plants and describes her style as "quiet observation".